# What Are You Prepared To Do?™

### FINDING PEACE BEYOND PERFORMANCE AND PAIN

## Mick Miller

First published 2025 in Australia by Mick Miller
Copyright © Mick Miller

www.mickmiller.com.au

Cataloguing-in-Publication Data: A catalogue record of this book
is available from the National Library of Australia.

ISBN: 978-0-646-72582-6

Subjects:
    Memoir


**Editing & Proofreading:** Sam Cooney
**Book Design:** Tony Gordon
**Manuscript Adviser:** Juliette Robertson
**Cover Design:** Ella Trapnell
**Cover Photo:** Mick Miller

# About The Author

Mick Miller is a high-performance enhancement
specialist who has coached Olympians,
world champions, and everyday people to achieve
extraordinary outcomes through mindset,
movement, and meaning.
His debut memoir *What Are You Prepared To Do?*
is a raw, powerful reflection on the cost of
chasing success without self-worth – and the healing
that begins when we finally stop running.

## Resounding international acclaim for the memoir *What Are You Prepared To Do?*

"In this book, Mick has opened up his heart and bared his soul. It's courageous, insightful, and inspiring. It's a must-read, a tribute to life being well-lived."

—Andy (Canada)

"Mick's writing is raw, authentic, and deeply moving – I felt like I was right there with him, and his story touched me in ways I'll never forget."

—Mike (Netherlands)

"You spent your life overcoming challenges, and what a wonderful job you did. I'm sure that your memoir will be inspirational to those who read it. You did a great job, Mick. Nothing is out of your reach."

—Chris (United States)

"Mick draws on a lifetime of highs and lows with honesty and heart. His unassuming wisdom and lived experience make this memoir not just his story, but a guide that challenges and supports readers to reflect on their own path."

—Viki & Mike (France)

"Unapologetically vulnerable, Mick shows that we should always look beyond the surface and respect the hidden journey that everyone is travelling. In doing so, he gives a gift of authenticity and generosity in his writing, which will undoubtedly help many to steer a course through confronting moments in life."

—Bec (London)

"As Plato is credited with saying, 'the unexamined life is not worth living.' I've known Mick for over 30 years, and he's always lived with a depth and honesty that most shy away from. This memoir doesn't just share his story – it dares you to look at your own and ask, *what are you prepared to do?*"

—Ashley (New Zealand)

"Mick's memoir is a powerful testament to resilience, showing how he turned personal, professional, and health challenges into wisdom. His story inspires readers to reflect on their own lives and recognise what they're prepared to do to rise above challenges and grow."

—Mitch (Australia)

# Table Of Contents

# *The Question That Changed Everything*

*"The question was never for them.*
*It was always for me."*

Over the years, I've received heaps of gifts and tokens from athletes, coaches, and parents, genuine expressions of gratitude for the campaigns we've endured together. Autographed jerseys, caps, handwritten notes, cards, and framed photos now sit quietly in a wardrobe at home. I'm deeply grateful for each of them. They speak to a life lived in the trenches of performance, discipline, setbacks, and breakthroughs.

At first, this gift presented no differently, just another framed picture, carefully wrapped in light-brown paper. I'd placed it on the passenger seat of my runabout for my short skim home across the open bay after a long, rewarding day with a team recently selected to represent Australia at the upcoming Olympics – no easy feat. They had endured the long grind, sacrifice, self-exploration, and relentless repetition. The layers upon layers; the often-frustrating systems of national sport. This campaign, like many before it, had demanded everything from them and me.

And yet, during the peaceful trip over the bay with only the hum of the trusty outboard, something about that day lingered.

These campaigns teach you plenty. Lessons I had not sought, but life has a way of handing you what you need, not what you expect. I learned more about patience. About understanding the art of listening – by allowing a couple of seconds to happen before you reply. I learned to simplify. To care more and control less. To stop talking so much and trust the silence. And I had begun to combine my feelings with my thinking.

It is simple to say.

Challenging to live.

For a long time, in parts of my life, I had not been living that way at all. That evening, after tying the dinghy to the pontoon, I unpacked the framed picture along with my well-worn backpack, and sat down on the edge of the ramp. The weathered timber was rough, the grain worn smooth in places from years of sun and salt. The sky bled shades of orange, pink, and purple that stretched endlessly across the horizon. A gentle breeze whispered secrets only the bay knew.

Two sea eagles circled high, their shadows flickering on the rippling water below as they hunted the last fish of the day. The local ferry chugged softly through the channel, its wake lapping quietly against the pontoon pilings. The driver caught my eye and offered a wave. I nodded back, sharing a brief moment of understanding between two men who knew the rhythms of this place. It was a quiet moment. A sacred one. Nothing was trying; everything was naturally happening.

A place where even I was invited to stop trying.

I broke the silence by unwrapping the noisy wrapping paper around the frame. The photograph was a brilliant shot of the team in full flight: fierce, composed, united. It was a beautiful gesture.

For some reason, I turned it over. There it was, scrawled in thick black ink:

**What are you prepared to do?**

I froze in place, breath catching, my heart suddenly heavier.

I had asked that question hundreds of times over the years. In locker rooms, on training grounds, in boardrooms. It was the cornerstone of what I delivered as a coach – how I lead, and how I live.

But now it was turning inward.

This time, it was not for anyone else. It was for me.

As the energy of the bay came over me, it brought me back to where that question was born. I remember repeating it silently at my younger brother's funeral, in that raw space. He had taken his own life; I became aware of how deeply those words had guided me. From a young, confused boy desperate for validation, to a man learning how to live from the heart. I truly believe my brother faced immense challenges trying to deliver that message to himself, only to be rejected again and again. Finally, he was free. Free from the emotional prisons we both knew too well. Free from the family still grappling with their pain, and who, for reasons of their own, chose not to attend his passing.

With my whole body present on the pontoon, wrapped in the fading light and the bay's quiet energy, the words repeated in my mind, churning something deep in my gut. Not pain. Not pride. Something more powerful. A reckoning.

My breath slowed, each inhale more relaxed. At that moment, surrounded by birds, tides, wind, ferries, and fading light, I felt the full weight settle over me. Everything I'd done … and everything I hadn't. Not as a coach. Not as a performer. As a person.

That feeling took me back to where the question was born: ambition, born from fear. The fierce drive to avoid loss at all costs.

I remember the service for him clearly. Sitting on a worn timber pew while the natural light shined through the stained glass as I grieved for him. The weight in the small, sunlit church. The air thick with melted candle wax, old wood, and faint incense. My loneliness seated beside me like a quiet mate. A single tear down my cheek, not loud, not dramatic, but carrying a message: *You cared. You showed up. You're still here.*

Few of his younger siblings had come. Our mother wasn't there. Our father had passed years earlier. None of his older siblings showed. I'd experienced this kind of loneliness before, but this time, I owned not just the tear, but everything it delivered to me. Ownership to me meant vulnerability. It meant choosing authenticity.

In that came a decision: to choose the intention with which I would move forward. I could follow the same path of judgment, resentment, and anger, or raise my standard. To follow the right path for me. To choose curiosity, compassion, authenticity, and love.

I offered this to them – a lifetime of healing, to my older siblings and parents. For where they were, who they were, for their truth, for their values and awareness which might never align with mine.

You know what? It was okay.

Sitting on that pontoon, held by the quiet energy of the bay, how I loved to feel that energy, and to allow it into me. I finally stopped chasing answers like needles in haystacks. I found the awareness to become still, found what had always been mine to discover and understand.

**"What are you prepared to do?"**

To truly grasp that question, I had to look back at my family's history. But to understand where it would take me, and why it still haunted me, I needed to go further back.

Back to the roots.

Back to the patterns I inherited.

And to move forward, I would need to become more curious, and less judgmental – of myself, and of them and their past. I had to become the magnet so all those needles would come to me.

That was the journey I chose. This was what I was prepared to do.

## Inherited Fires

*"What we don't heal, we hand down."*

Let me invite you into my birth parents' world, commencing with my mother's.

She had faced immense challenges of her own. Raised by a mother of her own who didn't know how to love her, in a home divided by step-parents and unmet expectations, she struggled to feel safe. Her stepmother found it difficult to connect with a child who wasn't hers, and her father, a tavern owner and heavy drinker, was emotionally absent. With no model of psychological safety, she turned deeply into faith. So deeply that she nearly became a nun.

Her armour was to debate. You didn't have to start; she could kick off an argument out of thin air. She would side-step direct questions like a seasoned politician, delivering what sounded right even if it missed the heart of what was being asked. It was her way of coping. Her survival strategy. Her attempt to be seen, heard, and ultimately loved.

My mother married young, and her husband, my biological father, also came from an upbringing of hardship. The youngest of seven, he was raised mostly by an older sister; his parents were exhausted by the time he arrived. He, too, found identity in faith – an altar boy who quickly realised that humour was his ticket to love. If he made people laugh, even at his own expense, which was often, he felt seen. That became his armour, and the military added layers of discipline.

When they married, they did the best they could with what they had. He took on various sales jobs, roles that suited his wit, storytelling, and people-pleasing nature. He had charm, hustle, and the ability to make people buy the products he was selling. But as with many in that world, the highs were high, and the lows were brutal. Still, he kept going.

My older sister arrived soon after, absorbing the full weight of their energy and effort. Neither parent had a college degree, just a set of tools passed down from their fractured upbringings: faith, duty, discipline. When I came along four years later, I was lucky to have her ahead of me. She was kind, loving, and deeply compassionate. My parents continued leading with what they knew: faith and fear. Like any child, I soaked it all in.

But that sponge absorbed both light and shadow.

Discipline in our house was delivered with an intensity shaped by the church and military. Punishments weren't just violent; they came with belts, cakes of soap in the mouth, and sermons involving sarcastic questions about whether the sin was mortal or carnal. Guilt became a house guest that never left; it seemed to have a permanent seat at the dinner table. While I endured this, my sister bore the brunt. She was the eldest, carrying the heaviest load.

I don't share this history in judgment. I share it because it matters.

Our parents never stopped to ask, *What am I prepared to do to become a better parent?* They didn't know how. They weren't taught. They led us the way they were led – by fear, tradition, and obligation. And while faith can be a guide, when weaponised, it becomes a leash.

There's a verse that matters here: "Do unto others as you would have them do unto you."

My parents treated themselves with guilt, fear, and silence, and so they treated us the same. Not out of cruelty, but out of repetition. That was their truth. That was their leadership.

I share all this because it plays a major part in this story. But beneath it all, beneath the fear, the patterns, the dysfunction, there's a universal truth: we all just wanted three simple things.

To love.

To be loved.

And to be happy while we're here.

Three simple things. Yet so often so difficult to truly experience. And I realised at that moment, while sitting on the pontoon, I wasn't just grateful for all those *What are you prepared to do?* experiences. I was finally ready to own them.

That's where this story begins.

Not at the top of a podium.

Not in the centre of a roaring crowd.

Here, surrounded by nature, avoiding the splinters on a timber pontoon which allows itself to float with the tide. A quiet place. A sacred one. Where a question I had asked of others was finally asked of me.

This book isn't about sport, or performance, or even cancer. It's about all the space between.

The part where you ask yourself who you are when no one's watching – and what you're truly prepared to do.

For yourself.

For the people you love.

For the life you want to live.

So, as I opened up to the universe, I asked myself, *Hey, mate … What are you prepared to do?*

So much of what shaped me wasn't shouted, but quietly passed down.

In glances.

In rules wrapped in religion.

In silences that echoed louder than words ever could.

My parents weren't bad people. They both were scorched and burned by fires they never lit. Without meaning to, they passed the flame to me. But the thing about inherited pain is this: if we don't name it, if we don't even know how to hold it, we repeat it. So I carried it, without realising how heavy it truly was.

This is where the echoes of their struggles became the wounds I tried to outrun as a small boy.

It's not a story of blame. It's a story of a boy trying to feel safe in a life built on fear. Then, without warning, everything shattered.

What happens when the ones meant to protect you become the reason you need protection?

## Chapter Three

# Band-aids Over Bullet Wounds

*"Children don't just grow up.*
*They grow around what hurts."*

I didn't know what to call it at the time. All I knew was that I didn't feel safe, and when a child doesn't feel safe, they don't feel loved.

I ached for peace, not presents.

For someone to ask, "Are you okay?" and mean it.

I learned early to listen more to what people didn't say than what they did. You can feel energy. You can sense when something's off.

The way a plate clatters too hard on the table.

The slam of a door that echoes longer than it should.

The smell of tension in the air – sharp, like burnt toast or the bleach under the sink.

Things got quieter at home, but not in the way anyone hoped. The kitchen radio, once humming with talkback chatter, fell silent. Dinners became dry reheats or hastily made sandwiches.

No conversation. Just the scraping of cutlery – that is, when we even used cutlery. Sometimes it was plastic forks and paper plates because all the others had been smashed during the fights my parents had.

One afternoon, as the shouting increased again, my mother's movements turned aggressive.

She spun suddenly, eyes glazed but furious.

Without warning, she grabbed a large kitchen knife and pressed it against her stomach. Her voice cracked into a scream as she lay down on the floor.

My heart launched into my throat. The world slowed.

I, along with my siblings, lunged at her. With all our energy, we wrestled the knife away.

I don't remember what I said, just that we were all crying and pleading. All of us were shaking and trembling so much that we could not speak.

I was eleven.

No child should ever feel the weight of their mother's life in their arms as they fight to keep her breathing.

After that day, things spiralled.

Dad became a ghost who was still visible for the next hour or so. His distance between all of us wasn't measured in kilometres, but in absence. He was still physically there, for a while, but emotionally he was long gone. His eyes didn't meet mine or the others. When they did, they seemed to look through us.

I don't think he knew how to stay, nor how to leave without breaking something. Though there wasn't much left that could be broken, emotionally, mentally, physically, or even spiritually.

All of us were shattered, hoping to put ourselves back together with what little we had, but there were a lot of pieces that had gone missing, never to be found again.

When he finally packed his bags, I helped carry one. The smaller bag was heavy with his belongings. I recall the strain of the weight made it hard to hang on to the sweaty handle; I had to use both my hands to move it. My whole body walked awkwardly under its load as the bag dug into the side of my thigh with each slow step.

Neither of us said much. We were both exhausted.

I felt so broken, not so much from the weight of the bag, but from what had happened to the family.

One final bag.

One final look.

No long hugs. No "I love you." Just a small boat disappearing across the bay with a person I wouldn't see again for a very long time.

I remember standing there, my hands still numb from gripping the suitcase. The sea breeze brushed my tears sideways.

I felt smaller than ever.

That's when I put the first invisible band-aid on.

I made people laugh so they wouldn't see I was hurting.

I worked hard so they'd think I was strong.

I volunteered for things no kid should take on, to feel useful.

I made fun of myself before others could.

I became the master of distraction.

Band-aids over bullet wounds.

At school, I wore a mask. If someone asked how I was doing, I'd throw out an "All good!" with a grin so wide it hurt my cheeks. But behind that smile was a boy flinching at raised voices, dreading the bell that meant it was time to go home.

I looked for approval wherever I could find it: teachers, coaches, neighbours.

I craved structure. I needed to know what was expected of me and how to win praise. Life doesn't pause when your world falls apart. It keeps moving, and so did I. That's when I found work. I started cleaning gutters.

The leaves and mud between my fingers felt oddly grounding. I'd perch high on a roof and look out over the landscape, the rolling hills, the water shimmering across the bay, hearing the occasional laughing kookaburra echoing through the trees.

It gave me a kind of peace.

I'd brush the sweat from my forehead, look down, and a neighbour would nod and say, "Good job, Mick."

Those words meant everything.

My hands scrubbed mud from gutters, but no one ever saw how hard I was scrubbing away at myself.

I cleaned the insides of water tanks until my hands smelled of dirt and rust. I remember the cool rush of the hose on hot days, the sting on my fingers, the sludge oozing between my toes as I stood barefoot on a tank's metal bottom. With every chore, I wasn't just earning a few bucks – I was earning my worth. Each job was a tiny anchor in a life that felt like it was drifting without direction.

I didn't understand it then, but I wasn't just asking, "How can I help?" I was asking, "Can you love me?"

The trauma didn't make me stronger – it made me quieter.

I spoke less.

I laughed louder.

I tried harder.

I carried shame that didn't belong to me.

And I became an expert at seeming okay. But every night, when the world went still, the silence reminded me of what was broken.

There was no one tucking me in.

No one asked how my day was.

It was just me, lying in the dark, replaying everything I was unable to fix.

I'd pull the blankets over my head, convincing

myself they created a safe zone, one where no one could see me, where, somehow, they would protect me as I lay in bed, quietly trying to patch myself up with emotional band-aids. One on top of another until the wounds disappeared from view.

But they never really healed, because the greatest pain a child carries isn't just the trauma – it's the silence they're forced to carry after.

I'd eventually spend years learning how to peel back those layers, but then, suppressing what needed addressing, and living in silence, was safer.

CHAPTER FOUR

# Anchored in the Storm

*"Sometimes we find peace*
*not in what saves us from the storm,*
*but in what steadies us while we're in it."*

Everything comes at a cost. I learned that, not through the physical work I was doing at eleven years old, but through the emotional wounds that had accumulated silently over the previous few years. Walking around with invisible injuries, scars we didn't know how to name, let alone heal. There was no counselling, no safe place to speak, no adults stepping in to help us make sense of it all. Only a tightrope in order to walk over emotional quicksand.

My older sister barely ate. Her migraines were crippling, her silence louder than any scream. It was a quiet, sustained cry for help that nobody seemed to hear. My younger siblings had their own trauma signals: bedwetting, separation anxiety, clinging fear.

We were a broken little tribe trying to look normal. And me? My body finally tapped out.

I'd always been strong and active, but suddenly, I was flattened by glandular fever. There were fevers, night sweats, dramatic weight loss, and bone-deep exhaustion that swallowed me whole. Sleep became something I feared. The nightmares and high temperatures were relentless; I floated helplessly in space, drifting away from Earth, from the tiny silhouette of our battered house. I'd clench to my bed, the one solid thing in a terrifying universe, terrified that everything I knew would vanish.

I missed months of school. No classes. No sport. No work. I needed time to allow my mind and body to reset.

I remember lying on the lounge one day, weak but slowly returning to life. The fridge was nearly empty. Mum was doing phone surveys, trying to hold things together financially. The parent who'd left wasn't helping, and the whole household felt like it was being held together with masking tape.

She walked into the room and looked at me – not gently, but with frustration. "How are you feeling?" she asked.

Before I could even open my mouth, she snapped, "You don't think I'm a good mother, do you?"

I hadn't said a word.

Suddenly, the guilt of being unwell was layered with something heavier: the guilt of being the emotional lightning rod for her pain. I didn't have the language for it at the time, but I felt like I was responsible – not only for my illness, but for her fragility. And behind that lay even deeper fears: Would there be dinner tonight? Would the power be cut? Were we going to be okay?

Eventually, the fever lifted, but something else had shifted, too. At school, I was behind. Way behind. My brain was slow to reboot. Reading and writing felt foreign. Spelling was like walking through mud, and although I knew my times tables, the new maths may as well have been written in another language. I started questioning everything: my intelligence, my worth, my place in the world. Most of my mates still had dads at home. They seemed steady, whereas I felt fractured, different. And guilty for it.

To cope, I leaned hard into humour and to being the good kid, the one who didn't cause problems, the one who made people laugh, the one who kept things light. What I didn't realise then was that I was sacrificing my voice so as to stay useful and liked. I was chasing belonging, looking for any way to feel seen, even if it meant disappearing parts of myself.

Eventually, I was strong enough to return to working odd jobs. But the moment that changed things came when I asked the owner of the local garbage barge who collected rubbish from the jetties scattered around the waterways if I could help during the school holidays.

He said no.

I kept asking.

Eventually, he agreed on one condition: I wouldn't be paid.

Back then, you could return soft drink bottles for five or ten cents, so he said I could keep whatever I made from collecting them.

The first garbage run was a baptism of fire: the smells, the ripped bags, the warm, sour sludge that seeped into my shoes and ran down my legs. It wasn't glamorous, but I loved it. The wind in my hair. The slap of waves against the hull. The chugging heartbeat of the old BMC Commodore diesel engine. The grit of the rope in my hands when I missed a throw and had to pull it back in. It was messy. It was challenging. It was perfect.

By the end of that first day, I'd earned more than three dollars, the most I'd ever made. I gave some to Mum and held onto the rest. But what stuck with me even more than the money was the way the people treated me. They didn't ask personal questions. They didn't pity me. They just welcomed me. I felt useful. I felt seen.

That job opened the door to another: the local ferry boat needed a helper to deliver the mail during the holidays. So, after my garbage shift, I'd jump onto the ferry and distribute letters and parcels for an hour or so.

Then came the school ferry. The girl who did the milk and newspaper run was in her final months of high school, so I put my hand up to succeed her. The school ferry picked up all the kids and delivered the milk and papers every school day. It was a wonderful way to start the day.

Now I had something I'd been missing: responsibility, trust, and belonging. The ferry drivers became my teachers – they showed me how to read tides and winds, tie off lines, helm in tight conditions, check the oil, and fuel the boats.

They gave me space to grow, and treated me like I mattered. The milk and paper run didn't stop for anything – not rain, not Christmas Day, not storms or hangovers. I'd have newspapers tucked under one arm, and bottles of milk in my hands, and as we came alongside the jetty, I'd leap ashore, make the drop, collect the empties, and jump back on.

I started learning the quirks of each jetty: which ones were slippery, which rocked in the swell, which had dogs waiting. I learned how wind direction shaped the water. I learned about tide flow, engine hums, and early morning stillness. My seamanship developed fast.

And those ferries … Those old wooden girls, they weren't just boats – they were characters. They creaked and groaned, smelling of salt, fuel, and old rope, but they were steady, familiar. They didn't lie. They didn't yell. They didn't change their moods. I trusted them. And that mattered, because the emotional chaos at home was still as bad as ever.

Eventually, I landed a paid weekend job as a deckhand. Some days were 12-hour hauls, others were short charters. I didn't care. I was out of the house, out of the emotional crossfire, into a world where things made sense. Work became my sanctuary.

The more I toiled, the more I felt valued. It was simple, and it worked. Looking back, I know how easily it could've gone the other way. I could've fallen into trouble, drugs, crime, anger. But my colleagues wouldn't have stood for that. They didn't need to say it. Their expectations were clear, and I didn't want to let them down.

What I gained was more than a wage. I gained independence. I got to ride through fog banks, tie off boats in storms, share chips and ice creams between runs, flirt awkwardly with pretty girls, and collect fares using my basic maths and a grin. But more than anything, I found a version of myself that felt real. Capable. Worthy.

That messy, working-class, salt-crusted lifestyle became my anchor. It gave me direction when everything else felt adrift.

Even now, I think about and reflect on the people who took the time to give me their attention. They weren't perfect; they had their shadows and scars. But they showed up. They taught me. They didn't ask me to explain myself, and they didn't try to fix me – they just made space.

They gave me something my world was missing:

kindness – without condition.

But even the calmest waters on the ferry run couldn't silence the storms I carried inside. And mine were only beginning to stir.

# The Right Kind of Silence

*"Children don't get to choose the adults they
depend on. They learn to survive them."*

Things don't always arrive when you're looking.
Sometimes, when you stop needing, stop grasping, let
go, then the right people appear. Quietly. Unassumingly.
At just the right time.

One afternoon, walking home from school, I passed
a man working in his front yard. He looked up, smiled,
and asked how my day had been. There was something
different about his energy: steady, warm, fully present. He
lived with his aging parents, one of whom had suffered a
stroke, and that same day, I found myself sitting with them
in the garden, sharing ice cream under a soft sky. From
the moment I stepped into that space, I felt something
unfamiliar, but deeply comforting: a quiet sense of safety.

He had a quiet spark, a calming presence, and a
knack for asking the kind of questions that made me feel

seen. I didn't catch him every day, but whenever I did, I walked away feeling like I mattered. He was a builder by trade, and a gifted drawer, good with his hands, brilliant with animals, and a natural at sport, though I wouldn't fully understand the extent of his talents until much later – he was too humble to say.

Next door lived another builder with a different personality: calm, confident, and quietly driven. He had a strong work ethic.

Soon, both households became safe havens for me. After school, I'd meet them at the job sites they were working at, helping sweep up, carry tools, or clean – just small ways to show my thanks. They were good men, and they treated me like I belonged. They made space for my jokes, my questions, my silence. Eventually, I met their parents and grandparents, who welcomed me with the same easy warmth. I stayed for barbecues. I watched footy on their TVs; we didn't have one at home. Those moments were like gold.

They taught me how to swing an axe. Handle a hammer. Move rocks underwater to build seawalls. Feed chooks. Clean paint brushes. Plant vegetables. They had gardens, sheds, animal pens, and skills that they shared with no agenda. They just gave me generosity.

Eventually, they met Mum. She was relieved I'd found steady male role models outside the ferry world.

One of them started doing some work at our place.

Our old water tank had rusted out, and he offered to install a new one. He dug footings, carted sand and gravel, and poured the slab. I'd race home from school to be near the job site. Anything to be around him. Anything to help.

He gradually became part of our lives. Sometimes he'd stay for dinner. Mum had been single for a couple of years, and I didn't think she'd ever meet anyone again. But this man, someone I already admired, began dating her.

One day, he told me he was going to marry my mum, and asked how I felt about this. A huge sigh of relief escaped me, and I told him I thought it would be great for all of us. I was excited to have a male parent back in my life. Someone to kick the footy and go fishing with, someone with whom to spend time in a father-son way. So they married, despite the ten-year age gap.

Everyone seemed fine with it except my eldest sister. I didn't understand why at the time, but now I know: that when people move into new relationships without healing what came before, they don't start fresh. They bring the weight of old wounds with them. Mum hadn't healed. None of us had. And, as I'd later learn, he had his own untended wounds.

Raised by his grandparents, my stepdad-to-be had been abandoned by his mother, who was caught in battles with alcohol, cigarettes, and a revolving door of men. He never knew his father. His grandparents, shaped by the Depression, were tough, pragmatic people. He grew up angry, and he poured that anger into the sport, then into teaching, then finally into building. After he married Mum, his grandparents welcomed us kids with open arms, but I didn't know the whole story back then. All I knew was that, at first, things felt good. I felt seen. Supported.

Slowly, things changed. The warmth drained from the air, like colour fading from an old photograph. The chats stopped. The smiles thinned.

I wasn't the kid this man welcomed anymore. I was the kid he now expected things from. The ice cream afternoons disappeared, as did kicking the footy, and going fishing. Expectations took their place. So did chores. So did pressure. So did silence.

Financial stress. Emotional tension. Constant demands.

We sold the family home and began moving from rental to rental. Meals still happened, but the atmosphere grew heavy, thick with sarcasm and short fuses.

Mum wanted stability; her new husband wanted freedom. They weren't aligned.

Then came a new baby, another brother for me. Plus I had a new Catholic school to attend – private, and far from home. This ended my weekday milk runs, but thankfully, I still had my weekend ferry shifts.

We moved into an old house that needed repairs. The rent was waived, but only if we repaired it ourselves.

We had chooks for eggs, and fancy show birds,

including my prize rooster, Randy. He was the most reliable alarm clock who made sure nobody slept in. And there were two goats which had to be milked every morning and night.

All this while I juggled school, ferry shifts, and endless adult expectations. There was always something: chopping wood for the stove; digging holes for the toilet pan; managing the rubbish; maintaining the boats.

There was no pocket money – just a quiet hope that dinner and a bed would still be there.

Strangely, I didn't mind the work, as it gave me something solid to hold onto. What wore me down weren't the tasks, but the criticism that came with them.

No matter what I did, it never seemed enough. My younger siblings felt it too, but I seemed to cop it the hardest. Even our new grandparents would sometimes urge my parents to ease up, but it didn't stick.

The adults around us weren't interested in growth, reflection, or kindness. No one ever asked, "What kind of example am I setting?"

Mum still drank and smoked daily. Her husband had his ritual beers. It was their way of coping. It was the structure.

There were meals. There was school. But there was no asking, "How are you feeling?" No one ever enquired, "How do you want to be treated?"

These kind of questions didn't exist in our world,

and so, I turned to the things that made sense: the goats, the chooks, the boats.

They all became my refuge. My rhythm. My proof of worth.

They never judged, never demanded. They just responded to care.

Late at night on weekends, I was sometimes asked to row our old timber dory across the bay to pick up my older sister after her dates. This was usually around midnight. I'd launch the boat beneath a sky of stars or soft moonlight, the silence broken only by the pull of the oars. If the conditions were right, the blades would glow with phosphorescence trails of blue-white magic skimming the surface. It felt sacred.

On the way back, sometimes me and my sister talked. Sometimes we didn't. But always, we understood the weight of that silence. She had given me so much over the years: her protection, her belief in me, her presence. And now, in this small ritual, I was giving something back. It was one of the only things I could do for her that felt meaningful. A way to say thank you without saying a word.

One afternoon, I came home to an empty house, and one of the goats was in labour. I had no idea what I was doing; I barely understood how babies were made. Me in my school uniform, covered in goat mess and hay, speaking the only goat language I could muster.

Sometimes she pushed. Sometimes I pulled. Somehow, together, we both figured it out.

By the time the third one arrived, we were a team. Three kids. Three.

It was one of the most incredible things I'd ever experienced. No one else in the area had ever delivered three goat kids, but I did. And no one said a word. No thanks, no "Well done." Just: "How are we going to afford another school blazer?"

I didn't even know how to reward myself, so I kept searching for praise. But it never came. How could it? My role models didn't know how to love themselves. Unless there was a drink in hand, they couldn't even feel.

Looking back, I know now: they weren't cruel. They were drowning. Worn out. Unable to lift themselves, let alone anyone else. Nothing was good enough. Not me. Not my siblings. Not even each other. I took the brunt of it, because sometimes parents push the hardest on the child in which they see the most potential. The one they secretly hope will become a better version of them. Eventually, something in someone was going to break. The only question was: "Who?"

But at that age, I didn't know how to break. All I knew was I had to keep going, because there weren't many other options.

That's what I found in the chores. The goats. The quiet. Not safety, exactly. Not love. But something that asked nothing of me. Something that didn't shout, shame, or sneer. Just the right kind of silence. But silence, no matter how confronting, can only hold so much. Eventually, the noise inside finds a way out.

# CHAPTER SIX

## Scattered Aces

*"You can be the life of the party and still feel alone. You can be surrounded by people and still feel unseen. You can be doing everything right and still not feel right inside."*

I rolled from teens into my twenties the same way I tackled each job: head down, work hard, say yes, get it done, stay busy. This was my shield, and also my reward system. If someone thought I was doing well or that I was capable, I felt useful. It was never about money or advancement; it was about being valued, noticed, and wanted.

But there was no roadmap. No clear direction. Emotionally, I was floating. I'd become a bit of a chameleon, someone who could blend in anywhere but didn't fully belong anywhere. I worked. I drank. I chased fun. I found it easy to talk with anyone and connect with them on the surface – by making them laugh, winning them over with energy and humour. But behind that was a boy still lost, still bruised, still trying to matter.

A girl leaned into me at a house party once, smiling, with soft eyes, genuinely interested. She touched my hand, whispered in my ear, and said she loved my stories. But I remember feeling and hearing … nothing. Not because I didn't like her – I did. But because I didn't know how to let her in. I looked around the room, made a joke, and took another drink. I could hold a conversation, but I couldn't hold her gaze for more than a few seconds. That kind of intimacy felt more dangerous than anything I'd ever faced on the water. The poor girl was seeking a solid connection; I could feel her frustration and confusion from her body language.

Looking back, I realise now how confusing it must've been for her to feel seen one moment then shut out the next. She didn't do anything wrong, she just met someone to whom she was attracted but who didn't yet know how to be open, real, or emotionally safe. I wasn't rejecting her – I was hiding from myself. It felt so ordinary doing this to girls; it felt comfortable in a way, yet so uncomfortable in another way.

I wasn't out looking to hurt anyone, but I know I did. I was in relationships that didn't go anywhere because I was unable to progress emotionally. I'd give what I could – a laugh, a story, a night out. But when things got too real, I'd step back, disappear, and find a reason to move on. I didn't have the language or the inner permission to explore my emotions, let alone share them.

Work was my constant. It consisted of long hours on boats, ferries, and wharves. I could lose myself in the rhythm and the responsibility. There was no ambiguity there, just jobs that had to be done and tides to follow.

There were mornings I'd drive the first ferry shift, and the bay would be like glass. Just me and the traffic of the seagulls, the engine low and steady, cutting through the mist. For those few minutes I could breathe while nature delivered something close to peace.

I'd sometimes sit on the deck after a shift, watching the sky change colour, and feel … nothing and everything all at once. The peace of the water was always there for me, but the peace inside was harder to find. I'd joke my way through pain, put on the mask, avoid conflict, keep people laughing, and keep them from looking too closely.

There was still no real emotional literacy in me. I wasn't cold, but I was careful. Carefully disconnected. And I wasn't deliberately cruel, but I was unavailable. I think I broke a few hearts during that time, not because I was a player, but because I was scared. Scared of being truly seen. Scared of the shame and the brokenness I still carried. I still believed I had to earn love, not just receive it, and the only way I knew to earn it was through service, action, and performance.

One night, I was driving the late ferry shift. The last passenger was a young man about my age who stood at the gangway, staring into the dark. We rode in silence.

As he got off, he nodded, and said, "Thanks, mate. Nice night to be invisible, hey?" I recall that this hit me like a three-punch combo. I nodded back, but my throat burned. I stood alone in the wheelhouse, the dim glow of the instruments the only light, the soft hum of the Gardner 6LX diesel the only sound. For the first time in years, I felt a tear fall down my cheek. Just one. I wiped it fast. No one could see that side of me. Not yet.

Some nights, I'd lie in my single bed in the tiny, rented boathouse, the plaster flaking from the ceiling, the old fridge that had no handle humming in the corner with barely anything inside, and I'd stare upward and wonder what it would feel like ... to feel safe. Not just from the world. But from myself.

The paint in that boathouse was yellowing and bubbled in one corner. The mattress was thin and creaky. Through the floorboards, where time had worn thin gaps, I could hear the tide lapping gently beneath me. The only light came when the moon shone through a broken blind. I didn't feel poor, just invisible. I'd drift to sleep wondering what kind of man I was becoming, and if I was the only one who felt like he'd missed the day they handed out the manual for life.

I didn't realise it then that I was carrying a thousand

unprocessed emotions. The unspoken guilt from Dad's leaving. The confusion around Mum's rage. The shame of never feeling worthy enough of anything. I buried it all in humour and work, in being everyone's mate, in keeping busy. If I was exhausted, I didn't have to feel.

They say when a deck of cards gets thrown into the air, some land face up, others down. Aces, kings, jokers, scattered. That was me. I was still in the game, still being dealt, but every part of me was scattered. I was still trying to build a life without a clear rulebook, hoping someone would come along and make sense of my cards, or that I'd eventually learn how to play them right, but the truth was, I wasn't ready. I wasn't even close. I could function, but I couldn't feel, not really. A quiet coldness had settled in, like I'd placed a heavy bag of ice across my chest. I didn't realise it then, but that numbness was slowly turning something tender into something hard. Into survival. And survival doesn't leave much room for connection. But life wasn't going to let me keep bluffing forever. A moment was coming that wouldn't just scatter my cards – it would force me to pick them up, one by one, and finally face what was written on them. The next hand I was dealt would threaten everything I thought I knew about loyalty, truth, and family.

CHAPTER SEVEN

# The Fence I Sat On

*"The truth does not change according to our ability to stomach it."* —Flannery O'Connor

While most of my mates were still figuring out who they wanted to be, I was already in the deep end, drowning under a tidal wave of bills, bricks, and expectations.

Turning twenty-one should've been a milestone worth celebrating, a chance to breathe, to reflect on where I'd come from, and the life I was about to build. Instead, it felt like I was holding my breath underwater, barely able to keep my head above the surface.

It was just days from my birthday, and so was a storm I hadn't seen coming.

By then, I was a qualified tradesman and a seasoned commercial boat driver. I'd bought out my parents' share of the family block, and alongside my stepfather, we were raising the first walls of my future. But every day was a relentless grind: two or three jobs, seven days a week. While my mates chased freedom and fun, I chased validation, the kind that comes from sweat, productivity, and the fleeting feeling of being enough.

I had a ferry license, but I still lacked a car driver's license. It became a joke among the locals, but beneath the banter I felt a gnawing fear: "Am I enough?" Each week felt like a race against failure, with the weight of financial pressure and a storm cloud hanging low and constant over my head.

The ferry was both my sanctuary and my trap. The salty tang of bay air clung to my skin as I gripped the wheel, the smooth bronze steady beneath my palms. The slow, rhythmic slap of water against the hull was the only soundtrack to early mornings and late nights that bled into one another. The pressure of bills pressed down like the fog rolling in off the water, damp, chilling and relentless. Every crossing was a battle against exhaustion, a fragile attempt to hold together a life fraying at the seams. Yet it was the one thing anchored me – literally. This little ferry that I drove across our bay was a lifeline for the community, and I respected that responsibility. But it also came with its social duties: birthdays, engagement parties, dinners, impromptu gatherings along the water's edge.

It was the perfect escape from looking inward.

I'd finish a night's last run, tie the ferry to whichever

jetty the party was at, slip into something halfway appropriate, and dive headfirst into the revelry. Most nights ended with me crashing wherever the party landed, only to drag myself back to the wheelhouse at dawn, foggy and worn, for another marathon of slow, looping crossings.

I can recall one pyjama party – a perfect storm of chaos, disguise, and personal release. The sky-blue pyjamas felt foreign against my skin, soft and loose like I was draped in someone else's vulnerability. The room pulsed with laughter, music bounced off the bay, and I enjoyed the sharp bite of cheap beer. The smell of spilled spirits mixed with sweat and cigarette smoke, thick and clinging to the air. My head spun, the world tilting unevenly as I stumbled through half-remembered conversations, each laugh and shouted toast a fragile mask over the ache curling in my chest. Every emotional band-aid was still stuck tight – but that night, they were stretched thin, threatening to tear with the slightest tug. Luckily, I had my sky-blue pyjamas on to protect me.

I set an alarm before passing out, somehow, but it was no match for the hangover and sleep-drug cocktail that swallowed me whole. I slept through the 6:15 a.m. ferry run, and the 7:15 one, too.

It wasn't until a mate, another ferry driver on the school run, saw the boat still tied up and knocked on my door that the fog started to lift. I woke to the sharp sting of sunlight on my body slicing through the curtains, the sheets twisted and clammy against parts of my skin. My head throbbed in sync with the creaking ceiling fan, where my crumpled uniform swung like a forgotten flag. The stale taste of last night's drinks and regret coated my mouth as I stumbled out the door, my heart hammering with a mix of dread and defiance. The ferry's deck was cold underfoot from the evening due to the familiar spray of saltwater hitting my face as I gripped the bronzed wheel in my threadbare pyjamas, a ghost piloting the morning run as the sound of the diesel motor penetrated my fragile head. Passengers smiled, oblivious to the battle raging behind my tired eyes.

That morning, I wasn't just carrying people across the bay; I was ferrying guilt, exhaustion, and a deepening ache inside me. But, like always, I smiled, kept the wheel steady, and made sure I suppressed everything under those pyjamas.

At twenty-one and living independently, my relationships with Mum and my siblings had improved; distance can sometimes bring clarity. I was nearly four years into carving a life of my own. Though my stepfather and I had just begun building the house together, our worlds barely overlapped beyond the construction site.

Building that home was monumental, a physical manifestation of everything I'd worked for. With close mates, I lugged timber and gear up that brutally steep block, knees burning, each step a reminder that commitment separates the curious from the true believers.

I was proud, even if I had no idea how to love myself beneath the sweat and grit.

One afternoon, Mum invited me over. Casual, she said. "Let's catch up." The sky outside was a cruel, immaculate blue without a puff of wind on the bay, mocking the storm gathering inside the room. The rich, bitter scent of freshly brewed coffee curled in the air, which would be warm and inviting on any other day, but beneath it, a different scent lingered, sharp and metallic, like cold steel pressing against the skin. My mother's eyes bore into me, a silent warning crackling in the quiet, the tension coiling so tight it squeezed the breath from my lungs. Every tick of the clock drummed like a countdown to something major about to happen.

She told me she was unhappy. I already knew that. But then she dropped a bombshell: my stepfather was interfering with my younger siblings.

Her words hit like a sledgehammer. Shock, confusion, disbelief vibrated throughout my whole body. I asked every question I could think of: "Are you sure? When? How?"

I'd seen the fractures between them: his drinking, her despair, the cold war of separate beds. But this? This accusation felt like a riddle wrapped in smoke. I wanted to hear from my siblings directly. She refused. The door to truth slammed shut.

Then the tone shifted. What began as a conversation became a command. I had to pick a side, and if I didn't choose hers—if I stayed neutral—I'd be cast out. I'd be exiled from the only family I had.

It wasn't a plea. It was an ultimatum.

Her gaze was ice, sharp and unyielding, boring into me like a knife twisting deep beneath my skin. The words cut through the room's heavy silence; harsh, raw, and final. The walls seemed to close in, the air thick and suffocating. My heart, pounded loud enough to drown out her voice. The weight of her threat settled deep in my bones. It wasn't just an ultimatum; it was a verdict. A death sentence for the family I thought I belonged to.

I left that house like a ghost walking through a minefield, dodging not only the invisible traps of mistrust but the flying shrapnel of pots, pans, dishes, and broken promises being thrown at me.

My chest was tight, my throat raw from holding back too much for too long. I didn't ease in, I broke.

As I stood in front of my stepfather, the words came fast, cracked and messy, spilling out between gulps of air, tears, and the snot I couldn't stop.

He didn't flinch. He just locked eyes with mine, like he'd braced for this moment.

"I need the truth," I said. "Please ... tell me what's going on."

His face barely moved. He let the silence stretch—thick, tense—before speaking. Calmly. Too calmly. "I didn't do anything," he said, denying the accusations. "I just moved out. Your mum … she's going through something. Something deep."

His voice didn't shake, and he never spoke ill of her, not once, but I saw the pain in his eyes.

Mum operated from a place where belief was truth, rallying allies like a general marshalling troops. Anyone not in her camp was the enemy, exiled without ceremony.

Days later, I watched detectives take my stepfather away. He was questioned, then released. No charges were filed. And he kept showing up at the building site, silent but resolute.

And Mum? She went to war. She contacted everyone she could, turning the local community into a battleground, tearing apart friendships with the force of a chainsaw.

There I was – on the fence. I refused to pick sides, but neutrality came at a price. I was caught between two worlds, both of them fractured and flawed. The house I had just started building was still rising, plank by plank, but inside me, walls were crumbling from heartbreak, not because I didn't care, but because I cared too much – about truth. About fairness. About loyalty. About myself.

That day, I learned the brutal cost of staying neutral. Sometimes, fairness makes you the enemy, but more than that, I was a young man just beginning to stand alone, even as the wind howled from every direction.

Sometimes, the hardest fences aren't the ones built between others; they're the ones we build inside ourselves. They are between loyalty and truth, love and justice, hope and pain. The cost of standing in the middle for me was the weight of loneliness, the ache of impossible choices, and the slow unravelling of certainty.

Yet, in that lonely place, I found the first fragile threads of my voice, one not shaped by others' battles, but forged in the fire of my resilience.

The house was still unfinished, and so was I. And maybe, that was exactly how it needed to be, because I thought staying neutral would save me. That truth would rise above the noise. But as the battle lines deepened and loyalties twisted into weapons, I began to realise something far more painful: this wasn't just a family falling apart. This was the slow destruction of who I was.

And the cost of not choosing a side? It meant losing myself entirely.

# Aliens Do Cry

*"Sometimes we must lose ourselves completely to discover who we truly are."*

For the next stretch of my life, I faced rage, blame, and cruelty on a scale I'd never known before. My mother made good on her promise to make my life a living hell.

The house got built, just scraped through on budget. My stepfather had stayed local, working through the court process while dragging his grief around like a heavy bag. His drinking worsened, but he still turned up, day after day, tools in hand, work boots laced, trying to hold onto something that felt like meaning.

There was now complete separation between me, my mother, and my siblings. Though she still lived nearby, the community chose sides, and I was an outcast.

A few months after my birthday, I received a large envelope at the post office. It had weight. I felt a flicker of excitement – maybe it was something official or meaningful.

Inside were the charred remains of my identity.

Burnt and blackened: my passport. My birth certificate. Paper once representing who I was, now nothing more than scorched ash. She'd posted it with no note – just her name scrawled on the back of the envelope.

In that moment, I wasn't just disowned – I was erased. I had no identity. No proof I even existed.

I cried that day. Not just for the documents. I cried for the boy who no longer had a mother. I cried for the silence of my siblings, now strangers. I cried for the suffocating truth: *How did it ever come to this?*

Years of fighting followed just so I could prove who I was. The legal system didn't care about the story behind the ashes, it just wanted paperwork. It became a grinding battle of re-establishing what had been destroyed.

And that was just the beginning. Mum started targeting me publicly. Some days, she'd board the local ferry I was working on, push past startled passengers, eyes blazing. "You're with a rapist!" she'd scream across the deck. "You've betrayed your own family!" Her words cut through the sea breeze, sharper than salt spray at forty knots. She spat in my face as I collected fares, right there, in front of tourists, locals, and kids holding ice cream. Then she'd barge into the wheelhouse, fist clenched, her voice rising like a storm surge. The warm spray of spit on my cheek was nothing compared to the fury in her eyes. That fury—raw, repressed, and deeply personal—hit harder than fists. Deeper than shame. It seeped past my skin, past the uniform stitched with my name, and sank into the soft places I had never let anyone see. It didn't just sting – it made me bleed, without a single cut to show for it.

My siblings avoided my eyes. Or, if they met them, it was to hurl insults, sometimes loud enough for strangers to hear.

I was still sitting on that same damn fence, being torn to pieces by the splinters.

Friends of hers, once friends of mine, turned their backs. Some threw words like daggers. Some threw fists.

The abuse finally stopped when she sold the house back to my stepfather and left the region with my siblings, but by then, the damage was done. I watched as my stepfather's grief took him under. He'd lost his son, his family, and eventually, himself. Alcohol swallowed him whole.

Strangely, he and I drew a little closer during that time. Broken recognises broken. The stress of it all aged everyone. It nearly buried my great-grandparents.

People I loved were slipping away, either physically or emotionally. And through it all, I still loved my mother. Not in a fairytale way, but in a raw, aching, impossible way. The kind of love that comes with barbed wire wrapped around it. I didn't realise then, but the issue was never the issue. It was how she behaved. The venom behind her grief. The fury behind her wounds. And I had no idea how to deal with any of it, so I did the only thing I knew how to do: I suppressed my emotions and continued working. I buried myself beneath the weight of the tasks that included manual labour, noise, and sweat. With each job, another layer pressed over the pain.

The local drinking tribe took me in without question. Their therapy was simple: a nod, a story, a laugh, a cold beer passed across the table. When I broke, they didn't flinch, they just poured another. They didn't know the full story. The thing was, neither did I. Yet they gave me their time, and that, sometimes, is everything.

Eventually, something shifted. I'd always thought change happened slowly, like erosion. But for me, it came through one simple, searing question: "What are you prepared to do – to change your life?"

I didn't have a plan. I was unfit, overweight, drank too much, and lived off garbage-type food. I was emotionally vacant, physically drained, and spiritually disconnected. I knew it had to stop.

I left the ferry job and the drinking culture with it. I started training at a local gym. I got fit, focused, honest with myself. The gym owner took a liking to me. I told him I wanted more than fitness – I wanted to work at the highest level, with Olympic athletes and pro teams.

He didn't laugh. He just asked, "What are you prepared to do?"

I said, "Anything." And I meant it.

I couldn't afford uni. I had a mortgage, and no savings. But I had hunger – and that, I'd learned, was sometimes enough.

I rented out a room in my house. Lived lean. Worked harder than I ever had. Every day started at 6 a.m. I cleaned the weights, re-racked equipment, shadowed the trainers, took notes. I studied late into the night. I learned anatomy, strapping, biomechanics, and emotional support. I wasn't chasing a job, I was investing in my destiny.

At the end of each work day, the gym owner would give me a made-up injury scenario. A hypothetical athlete, a deadline, and a challenge: fix them, not just physically, but emotionally and psychologically, on paper, by morning.

I'd ride home fast through the rain, cook on the stove, highlighter in hand, pages spread across the bench. I'd hand-write my reports, crawl into bed after midnight, then rise again before dawn.

This went on every day for eighteen months.

He grilled me, challenged every answer, but he never belittled me. He wanted me to own what I knew and to be better than him.

That was rare. That was gold.

I studied every course I could afford. Met with lecturers, sat front row, took notes. Volunteered. Connected with new people, new energy, and a new tribe. I helped train national-level athletes, and even worked with an Olympian. Slowly, I built not just skill, but belief.

The support from my stepfather was paper-thin. "You're not good enough," he would say. "You won't make a living from this."

I don't know if he said these things out of fear, jealousy, or pain. Maybe all three. But it cut me.

Even as I built something new, I still craved his approval. I wasn't close to loving myself yet – not even on the radar. I was still people-pleasing. I was still performing. I was still patching up wounds with busyness and band-aids. My gym bag had literal tape for sore joints, but the real pain was internal, unspoken, and untreated.

Helping others made me feel useful, but it didn't heal the grief inside. What I really needed was emotional surgery. To go inward, to stop suppressing, to stop surviving. Instead, I just kept moving, because stillness scared me more than pain ever did.

But even as I trained harder, lifted heavier, and built the body I thought might carry me forward, there was still a boy inside me, grieving, gasping for breath, trying to row his way out of a storm far older than he understood.

Soon, I'd have to find a new vessel to carry that weight. Something with no engine. No shelter. Just water … and truth. And in that truth, I would discover what I was really made of.

## Chapter Nine

# The Strokes That Counted

*"It's not the size of the dog in the fight,*
*it's the size of the fight in the dog."* —Mark Twain

The gym had made me strong – not just in body, but in will. And I needed it, because I was full – of unspent anger, grief, defiance, emotions that had nowhere to go, no safe outlet, no name. It was like having a furnace roaring inside me with the chimney sealed shut. I knew if I didn't move that fire somewhere constructive, it would burn me from the inside out.

So I did what I'd always done when things got too loud in my head: I made a list, writing down the five most energy-demanding sports in the world. Each one is a crucible. I broke them down, studied and researched them, and tried to figure out which one might meet me where I was: raw, unsure, but desperate to channel this energy into something honest.

As fate would have it, one of them, still-water rowing, found me before I could pick. I had learnt from a young age how to row a timber dory around the bay, so I understood the basics, but still-water rowing done in a racing shell was a level up from what I had experienced.

So, I leaned in. I showed up at the local rowing club with a heart full of fire and no idea what I was doing in that type of boat. I wanted to learn to row a single scull – a sleek, twitchy little boat, barely wider than your backside. Two oars, one sliding seat, no engine. Just you, the water, and the truth. It's the kind of boat that tells you exactly who you are.

They took one look at me and laughed, saying I was "Too short," "Too small," "Too light." Saying to me: "Don't waste your time."

It wasn't even malicious. Just matter-of-fact, like they were describing the weather. They'd seen Olympians walk through their sheds: six-foot-plus praying mantises with thighs like tree trunks and with hearts the size of a racehorse. I didn't fit the mould. I barely fit the boat.

I'd been here before, rejected by people who thought they knew what I was capable of, so I was well-rehearsed in this kind of dismissal. The sting wasn't new, but this time, something inside me didn't absorb it. This time, I pushed back – quietly, internally, but it was real. For years, I'd been letting other people narrate my story, telling me what I couldn't be, what I wasn't, who I'd never become.

And somewhere along the line, I'd stopped questioning them, but now, standing there on that dock, I decided to question everything. That's when I heard it again – my question: "What are you prepared to do?"

I found a retired local coach who saw something in me – maybe not potential, but commitment. He said, "I can teach you how to row. Then we'll find someone to teach you how to race."

So we started, just the two of us. In rain, hail, or sun that could peel your skin off. Days when the bay was glassy, and days when the wind punched sideways and turned the boat into a bathtub. I rowed through it all. I fell out more times than I care to admit. My coach, he never flinched. He patiently just waited for me to climb back in the rowing shell, drenched and shivering, and then we'd keep going. And I began to feel something I hadn't in a long time: respect for myself.

Once he felt I had the basics, he handed me over to someone else – a man with Olympic medals and a no-bullshit attitude. This new coach would say, "I can teach you how to race. But let's be honest, I don't expect you to win." He wasn't being cruel, he was being real.

I joined his small squad of experienced scullers, every one of them with big bodies, big lungs, and even bigger expectations.

I didn't come in with expectations – I came in with intentions: to earn a seat, to earn respect, to see if, in the middle of all that power, noise and sweat, I could still find a rhythm that was mine.

Racing training was different. Short, savage bursts. Minimal rest. High rating intervals that made your vision go white. By the end of some sessions, we could barely lift the boat off the water, let alone our bodies out of the shell. I kept showing up.

I knew I wasn't built for this, but I also knew I was made for this. The season came. Every weekend, I lined up, pushed hard, and watched as the field pulled away after the first 500 metres.

My fellow racers always waited for me at the finish line. Smiling, encouraging, polite. And I always came in last. But I learned.

It wasn't just about rowing. It was about campaigning. About discipline. This was about enduring the middle of something you know you might never win. And the fitness I gained was extraordinary.

Then came the final race of the season.

I showed up that morning with no illusions, no expectations. Just intentions: to give everything, like always. And I figured I'd come last, like always.

The usual rituals played out: greetings, gear checks, a few handshakes. Then something in the air shifted. I smelt it: a faint salt-crackled shift. The kind that gives no warning except to those who know.

I'd grown aware of this sign in my time on the bay. I

knew it well. A 'southerly buster' was coming.

The others didn't notice. They were too busy warming up and adjusting their footplates and focusing on power output.

Me? I braced.

*Bang!* The starter's gun cracked like a whip, and we were off.

The first 500 metres was the same story: I held my own. Legs burning. Arms strong. Core locked in.

And then it hit.

The southerly exploded across the bay like a fist. The flat water turned into a snarl of white caps. Boats flipped. Rowers panicked.

But not me. I'd trained in this. This wasn't rowing anymore, but seamanship. And that was my language.

While others fought to stay afloat, I rowed with everything I had. Waves slammed over the bow, cold and relentless, soaking me to the bone. The sliding seat jammed hard beneath me, throwing off my rhythm. My oars were buried deep in the churning water, caught and stuck, but I adjusted, muscles burning, breath ragged. I trusted every shred of training and instinct I'd earned.

One by one, I passed them, each surge pushing me closer to the edge of what I thought was now possible.

I crossed the finish line first, heart pounding, muscles and lungs screaming. Saltwater dripped into my eyes, stinging sharply. My body trembled from the effort, exhausted but alive, and my cheeky grin broke through the pain; I felt the fierce, wild joy of victory. For the first time, I waited at the finish line, grateful and quietly clapping as the rest came in, soaked and spent.

I'd won my first—and only—rowing race. And it was enough. Because it wasn't about the win. It was about that moment, when everything I'd endured, everything I'd been told I wasn't, everything I feared, collided with who I was and who I was becoming.

That night at the clubhouse, I celebrated with those close personal friends who had supported me. A few established Olympic rowers came over and shook my hand – not just for the win, but for sticking with it, for showing up, for giving it a red-hot crack when the odds said no.

I knew I was never going to be an Olympic rower, but I'd become something else. Someone who didn't back down when the storm hit.

Was I a good rower? Maybe. For a slick 500 metres.

Was I everything they said I wasn't? Not in their eyes.

But in mine? Hell yes.

Was it a fluke? Who cares? A win's a win.

They told me I couldn't, but I didn't listen. The storm did, and it cleared the path. That race may have been the end of my season, but it lit the fuse on something much bigger, because next time, it wouldn't be calm water I'd be facing. It would be an open ocean. Fumes. Fear. Vomit. And a job that would test more than just my lungs.

# Baptism by Water, Spew, and Engine Fumes

*"You don't drown by falling in the water.
You drown by staying there."* —Edwin Louis Cole

The gym and rowing apprenticeship wasn't over; it was evolving. I wasn't a student anymore – I was stepping out as a tradesman. It was time to leave the safe, known space of the little gym where I had first been forged and take my place in the unpredictable, high-stakes world of professional sport. The house was rented, my bag was packed, and I was ready to put everything I'd built into motion and find out if I could deliver.

My first break came from a women's outrigger canoe crew preparing for the iconic Moloka'i Channel Race, a brutal six-to-seven-hour paddle across the open ocean in a six-person canoe. This was no Sunday splash. This was war with water.

Each team rotated between six paddlers in the

boat and six reserves, the latter who'd leap from a nearby escort vessel into the open sea and swap places mid-race. The changeovers happened on the move: tired paddlers dove out and fresh ones climbed in. It was pure chaos, surrounded by wind and crashing waves, combined with precision teamwork.

The coach and I were on the escort boat, a 30-footer with a half cabin for the driver and two thundering 300-horsepower outboards bolted to the stern. My job? Keep the resting paddlers functioning: feed them, hydrate them, stretch their locked-up hips, rub cramping backs, fire up their minds, calm their panic, and keep them sharp – until it was time for their next leap into the blue ocean. This rotation happened every 12 to 15 minutes, and continued for seven hours.

The race day exploded with heat – the Hawaiian sun could've melted concrete. Canoe decks shimmered under 25-knot winds. The Pacific heaved with liquid mountains, rolling through with force and rhythm, a living reminder of who was really in charge.

Within 30 minutes, the horror started. The pitch of the boat, the fumes of the outboard engines, the relentless swell, plus a cocktail of nervous energy and last night's pasta: the self-draining cockpit couldn't keep up. Seawater and vomit sloshed around my ankles, thick with emotion and fear.

Every twelve minutes, a wave of drenched,

exhausted bodies clambered aboard. I braced as they collapsed, crying, dry-heaving, cramping. I rubbed down limbs, mopped sweat, held trembling hands, whispered motivation, and kept my footing as the boat tossed like a bottle in a cyclone.

The coach, loud, proud and relentless, barked orders over the wind and waves. He didn't care about comfort, he cared about results. So did I. This wasn't a test. This was the job. This was the crucible. And I didn't flinch.

The team finished in the top ten from more than a hundred crews. I was green, unproven, but I'd delivered. And in the middle of the chaos, I felt it: *I belong here.* I added value, I held my line under pressure, I backed myself. Afterwards, the coach offered me recognition: a nod, and some money. But I felt uncomfortable taking it, and I squirmed under the praise. It felt foreign, like I didn't have the right to accept his offer. A voice in me whispered, "Don't get ahead of yourself. You are on the right path. You still have a long way to go ." That voice sounded like my past. The same one that made praise feel conditional. I had heard this many times before. At this time, I was under-resourced in terms of feeling comfortable celebrating myself. In this moment of feeling uncomfortable within, I suppressed the celebration by burying it under the saltwater, sweat, and my inner silence.

The coach didn't hesitate – he asked me back the following weekend, this time with the men's team. The same chaos, same pressure. More spew, more seawater. And the same result: I delivered, and I got paid. I was officially in the game.

The outrigger crews flew home. I stayed and picked up work with the state kayak coach, and I scored hours in a luxury hotel gym by the beach. There was a free staff cafeteria, so I ate like a king, flashing my ID even on days off to stretch my budget. In return, I volunteered for the coach, and he offered free rent nearby. It was a barter system. Sweat for stability.

I had my pushbike, my island loop. Sunsets, waves, moonrises. A postcard life. But I knew paradise wasn't the destination. It was a pit stop. It was a fantastic training ground, in which I was grateful to have had the experience.

That question kept tugging at me: What are you prepared to do?

An opportunity came up in the U.S., in a pre-Olympic training environment. I said yes. It felt like the next leap. I bought a one-way ticket.

It lasted two days.

I showed up, ready to work. The welcome was warm, until it wasn't. I was told I had the job, and then, without warning, I didn't. No explanation. No fallback. Just silence.

I figured maybe the funding for an overseas coach had fallen through – or more likely, they'd found someone local to fill the spot.

This was my first real taste of what I'd later learn was common in Olympic circles: plenty of ambition, plenty of pressure, and no shortage of politics. In less than 48 hours, I went from being a professional coach to sleeping on a park bench, living off $1.99 bowls of fried rice. No car, no contacts, no roof. Just my bag, and my belief.

The first night, I lay on a splintered bench beneath a flickering streetlamp that had lured every moth in the area. With my hoodie pulled tight, I was trying to convince myself I wasn't homeless, just between homes. I'd laid out my only towel on the bench to make it more comfortable, to dull some of the pain, but it didn't help much. Under the bench next to my bag was the takeaway container with the plastic fork snapped at the handle. The smell lingered: soy, oil, a little sadness mixed in with a few tears.

I watched the world move on in a different direction without me. Headlights passed on the highway nearby like glow lights of warmth I couldn't touch. Every car was going somewhere. I wasn't. Not yet. I felt the weight of disappointment, the sting of uncertainty. My thoughts were louder than the traffic. How did I end up here? Had I pushed too hard? Did I chase the wrong dream? At times, I was scared. Uncomfortable. Exposed. But underneath it all, something still burned – a stubborn spark that kept me warm and refused to go out. "You've still got something to offer," I told myself. "You need to connect with the team that needs it."

Then the question came – not as a slogan, not as inspiration, but as a challenge to survive: What are you prepared to do now?

I didn't break. I pivoted.

The next morning, I wiped the sleep from my eyes, slung my bag over my shoulder, and stuck out my thumb on the edge of a freeway I couldn't name. I had an idea where I was headed: south, towards that team. Anything. A foot in the door. A new shot. And that's when I landed in an Australian team's America's Cup campaign.

Through a rowing contact, I was given a sliver of a chance. It wasn't glamorous, and it wasn't coaching, not yet. But I got in, just. And once I was through the door, I worked like hell to stay there.

I became everything: a security guard, a trainer, a boat builder, a morale guy, all alongside Olympic medallists and world champions. I watched. I listened. I showed up. I delivered.

By then, I'd learned something most people never do: sometimes your dream doesn't need applause – just persistence.

Eventually, they gave me a blazer, an Australian team blazer with the coat of arms. To most, it was a jacket. To me, it was my badge of honour.

I called my stepfather with excitement: "Hey … I made it. A national team. Got the blazer."

His response? "Don't forget, you're no better than

anyone else." And he hung up.

I stared at the phone, gut-punched, but not surprised. I had climbed a mountain, and the man I still sought approval from had barely noticed.

That blazer went into my bag. Later, when I returned home, I put the blazer in the wardrobe. Still crisp, still clean, and still a small part of me waiting to feel worthy enough to wear it.

That America's Cip campaign lasted nearly a year. When it ended, I knew: it was time to go home. But I was still learning how to dry off. I hadn't drowned, I'd swum through it, but I was still learning how to dry off.

And something inside me was beginning to stir, something quieter than pride, but deeper than survival. I was no longer asking *if* I could do it. I was starting to wonder *why* I still needed to.

I didn't know it yet, but the next chapter wasn't going to test my strength. It was going to test my truth.

And for the first time, I wasn't just chasing success. I was chasing myself.

~•~

## Chapter Eleven

# Let's Go and Get Them

*"When we are no longer able to change a situation,
we are challenged to change ourselves."*
—Viktor E. Frankl

Slipping off the jumbo jet and hearing 'I Still Call Australia Home' playing as we disembarked was a great feeling. I'd been away for about sixteen months, and felt like I hadn't just added value to some elite teams – I'd earned a symbolic green-and-gold blazer along the way.

Reality hit hard. I'd landed home just as the country had slipped into a recession, and most professional sporting seasons were already kicking off, which meant there weren't many opportunities to walk straight into. So I picked up labouring work with my stepfather; he had now settled in the family home with his new partner. Had he addressed some of his issues? I wasn't sure, and really, it wasn't my business. There was still a wall between us. He lived only a few doors away emotionally, but we didn't visit each other much. What I did discover was that digging trenches and shifting endless amounts of building material from one site to another was bloody hard work. It gave me plenty of time to think. I was grateful, it helped with the mortgage, but I wasn't working with a purpose. I was clocking in for a pay packet. I started asking myself again: What are you prepared to do? It had become more than a question – it was a compass. A quiet companion that held me accountable when no one else was watching.

Eventually, I picked up the phone and called a few of the lecturers who'd once taught me and supported my journey. That led to a gig with a first-grade rugby league team that needed a strapper and sports therapist for training sessions and game days. This was more like it. The environment was electric. I was in my element, delivering my skill set in a high-performance environment again, and I loved it.

Getting to training was another story. Two buses and a long walk to make it there. The team trained late three nights a week near the city, and getting home was even tougher. Money was tight. Some nights I hitchhiked. That usually worked, unless it was raining – then no one wanted a soaked strapper in their car. On those nights, I walked the full 30 kilometres home, crawling into bed just before dawn. If I had enough for a one-way fare, I only had to walk six.

Those walks became my ritual, especially in the

rain, water slipping down my back, soaking my socks, squishing between my butt cheeks. It was uncomfortable, but it gave me space to think. To harden. To ask the question over and over like a quiet war cry: What are you prepared to do?

That question kept me moving when everything else said "stop." With every soaked step, I was building something – not just a career, but a kind of conviction. An internal engine that only I could see.

I was becoming the man I wanted to be. One drenched, defiant step at a time. And if I'm honest, the rain sometimes felt like it was washing away the doubt, though I still didn't know how to speak out loud.

The season went well. The team performed, and I knew doors would open soon. They did, through a mate from the rowing club who let me know the state team was looking for someone with my background. I arrived at the interview and was met by a six-foot-six, two-time Olympic gold medallist from East Germany. He had an intense presence: organised, direct, and obsessed with elite outcomes. He was the new state rowing coach, and he was here to win.

He scanned my résumé. He skipped straight past the prestigious teams I'd worked with, including the Australian America's Cup campaign, and stopped at the last item: a short stint working behind the bar at a nightclub. "Do you drink?" he asked in that thick German-English accent.

"You can never trust a man who doesn't drink." I smiled.

It was lucky for me that he didn't ask *what* I drank.

He gave me the job. A week later, I was travelling interstate with the team. I was excited. I'd been *given* a new opportunity, but I'd *earned* it.

From day one, expectations were black-and-white: organise the medical rooms, prep the massage tables, have all the strapping ready, and keep everything spotless. Then came his real message: "If I have to speak to you about anything, it means you're not doing your job. The less I say to you, the better. Keep the medical room spotless. And if you're late, you don't have a job. Do you fully understand?" I nodded. Loud and clear. That was the beginning of a long and mutual respect.

A few days later, we were preparing for the national titles. The rowers and I were finding our rhythm. The days were long and challenging, both physically and mentally intense, and I loved it. I felt like I was *exactly* where I was supposed to be. Then came an odd task: the coach told me to head into town and buy as much bicarbonate soda as I could find, and some empty capsules, no questions asked. So I didn't ask, I just hit the chemists and supermarkets and cleared out their entire supply.

That night, I sat watching late-night TV, filling capsule after capsule with bicarb. Powder was everywhere: on the bench, my clothes, my face. Then came the knock.

Three plainclothes detectives. They scanned the

white powder, the capsules, the mess, and started firing questions: "Why did you buy out the town's supply of bicarbonate soda?" "What are you putting in those capsules?" "What are you planning to do with them?"

They took samples. There were two options: get taken in for further questioning, or go and wake the six-foot-six German coach I'd only just started working with.

I knocked on his door. He answered in a robe, wide awake. I said it was urgent and team-related. He didn't ask, just followed. I was half-expecting him to bring his stopwatch.

The look on the detectives' faces when he ducked through the doorway was priceless. With a few sharp lines in that accent, he waved them off and sent them packing.

Lucky for me, a night in a jail cell has never been on my bucket list. That moment told me everything I needed to know: this guy understood the system, and he'd go to bat for his people. I was in the right place. I'm not a sports scientist, but from my understanding, bicarbonate soda helps reduce lactic acid during intense exertion. It's natural; it's not a drug. There were about fifty athletes on that state team. Over the next seven days, I rubbed down bodies, strapped ankles, lifted morale, calmed nerves, hyped energy, and contributed with quiet words when needed. I gave everything, and the team performed brilliantly.

From there, we moved into national selection

regattas across the country. This is where the culling began. The elite would be picked for an international campaign in Europe.

I travelled with them from state to state for the next few months. When the national team of sixty was finally chosen, I was selected by the governing body to join the medical staff on tour. That tour would last nearly three months. We'd race against the best in the world.

All the risk. All the digging. All the walking in the rain. All the times asking myself "What are you prepared to do?" It had paid off.

I'd already represented my country in sailing. Now I had the chance to do it again in rowing. I was proud. Quietly, deeply proud.

I'd worked hard and earned my place, and I wanted to share that with my stepfather. I told him the news, hoping for a flicker of something. A nod. A "Well done." Even a grunt. But there was nothing, just that same unreadable face. No recognition. No spark of connection. That silence sat heavier than words ever could.

I told myself it didn't matter, but it did. I was aware that my validation-seeking continued, but I didn't have the resources to change it. His validation wouldn't have changed my path, but it might've calmed the waters. Some men build fences instead of bridges, though maybe then he didn't have the tools for either. Maybe he never did.

I poured myself into the team. I wasn't just rubbing

down bodies anymore; I was in the room, sitting in on medical briefings, physio consults, and coaching strategy meetings. I started running the stretching sessions, supervising the weights room, leading boxing drills, skipping sessions, Swiss ball routines, and the full program. And somewhere in all that sweat and structure, I started investing in myself. Not in a flashy, self-help way, just quietly, consistently. I wasn't sure if it was the right investment, but it was an investment, and for once, it felt like it was mine.

Every morning, no matter what bed I woke up in or what country I was in when my feet hit the ground, I'd say out loud, "Let's go and get them – before they come and get us." It sounded motivating. And it worked, for a while. *Us* being the team. *Them* being everyone else.

Deep down, I knew it wasn't a healthy way to operate. It was pure ego. The ego lives in the past, in the future, and in fear. Another sidestep, more avoidance. A green-and-gold one. Suppressing the fear that still lived inside me, but I wasn't ready to take off what was covering that emotion and feeling just yet, as it was too raw to face. I was still surviving. Still proving. Still asking: What are you prepared to do?

This team, this chance, this journey, it mattered. It mattered deeply. But it wasn't the destination, just another step on the way home. And I was beginning to understand something I hadn't realised before: it wasn't just about how hard I was prepared to work, but about how honest I was prepared to be with myself.

I was winning on paper, making progress, living the kind of life others admired, but winning and healing aren't the same thing.

I'd stepped onto the world stage again, this time in rowing. I was in the room, I was part of the system. I was contributing, growing, and performing. And while the world clapped around me, I quietly wondered how long I could keep outrunning what I hadn't yet faced.

Somewhere inside, I still hadn't come home to myself.

I could feel the band-aids rubbing beneath my Australian uniform, but for the first time, I'd started asking the deeper questions. And maybe, just maybe, I was finally ready to listen for the answers.

# CHAPTER TWELVE

## The Noise I Mistook for Worth

*"I was always running. Always trying.*
*But no one ever told me I could just stop and be."*
—Brianna Wiest, *The Silence After the Applause*

The career door had fully opened. What began with elite rowers and sailing teams had evolved into a modest high-performing strength and conditioning business based at the local yacht club. It wasn't much—just a squat rack, a bench, some weights, a rowing machine, and a punching bag—but it had purpose, grit, and a heartbeat. I was proud of it. More than that, I was grateful the club had given me the space.

Within a year, I was coaching state, national, and world champions in both sailing and rowing. The word spread. The governing body of sport took notice. A scholarship followed. Before long, I was working with both state and national teams.

That's when the national team bosses sat me down.

"There's a pathway here if you want it," one of them said. "But just know, it's a very unique club. The Five Circles Club. And this club comes first." No fluff, no warm-up, just clarity. Don't ask to leave for a wedding, a birthday, or even a funeral if you're overseas with the team. Do you fully understand?

Then came the line that stuck: "In this club, ninety-nine per cent of married coaches end up divorced. This life will consume you. Choose wisely." I didn't flinch, just nodded. Not because I didn't hear the warning, but because part of me welcomed it.

I bought in fully, and wore it like armour. On the surface, I was saying yes to high performance, but underneath, I was saying no to something else entirely: to the grief I hadn't grieved, to the questions I didn't want to answer, to the parts of me I wasn't ready to sit with.

The Five Circles Club offered more than a career – it gave me something to disappear into. A place to stay busy. A system where performance could drown out pain. The stopwatch became my compass, and performance my god.

I never stopped. When one campaign ended, another began. Rowing season bled into sailing. When the sailors were overseas, I trained cancer survivors. In between, I studied, lectured, trained myself, and ran the business. Every minute was accounted for. There was no space for silence, no space for stillness, and no space for me.

I tried to show up in relationships, but they were always second. Eventually, the person would leave, and each time, the echo was the same: *abandonment, rejection, not enough.* The pain was ancient. Familiar. I'd smother it with new goals, fresh clients, and louder applause. Layer after layer, I added more emotional resources so I could keep suppressing my emotions.

The career gave me something I hadn't realised I was starving for: safety. Not from danger, but from introspection. If I stayed busy enough, I didn't have to ask the questions that scared me. I didn't have to face shame or heartbreak. I didn't have to sit with the truth that beneath the competence was a boy still chasing his parents' approval, still desperate to be seen.

I overpromised and underdelivered emotionally. I wanted a connection, but I didn't know how to hold it. So when someone walked away, I collapsed inward. *I'm not enough. I'm not lovable.* And then I'd go harder. Lift heavier. Train longer. Coach more.

From the outside, I was killing it. Fit, composed, driven. But underneath? I was exhausted. I was an impostor. Still trying to prove something I couldn't quite name.

Olympic campaigns don't wait for emotional meltdowns. There's no pause button for grief. And for me, vulnerability felt like failure. Asking for help wasn't an option.

I never once asked myself the question I now pose to others: "What are you prepared to do?"

I was the fixer. The strong one. The one people leaned on. How could I possibly admit I was empty inside? So I kept performing. The ego loved the applause, and the applause kept the walls up.

Meanwhile, my stepfather had started a new family: a beautiful partner, two young children. Our relationship was cordial but distant. No deep chats. No calls to check in. The postcards I sent from around the world were rarely acknowledged.

I kept trying to earn his approval. I never received this from my biological parents, and some part of me believed that if I just achieved enough, if I was impressive enough, he might say the words I longed to hear: "Mate, I'm proud of you." But they never came. He gave me advice at times, mostly when I asked for it, and I respected that he had his own life, but deep down, I still wanted more.

Then came the call.

An east coast low had drenched the coastline for days. They'd just welcomed another baby, and though I wasn't part of their family unit anymore, I was happy for them. Still, something didn't feel right. I'd heard he'd been spending more time with the local drinking community. Newborn life hits everyone differently. Our last conversation had nothing to do with the new baby – it was about real estate. "You won't lose on a waterfront on the east coast," he'd said. "Can you make it happen?"

I'd just slipped into bed at around 8 p.m. The phone rang. It was his partner: "There's been an accident. Come to the house straight away."

I raced to the house. As soon as I saw the crowd, the flashing lights, the helicopter blades chopping through the night sky, I knew. He'd been coming home when his boat struck a floating barge.

He didn't make it. He'd drowned.

The town was gutted. He wasn't just known; he was *woven* into the local fabric. You could feel the loss hanging in the air like salt. I was already on shaky ground. I'd just come out of a long relationship, and emotionally, I was raw. But this? This cracked something I didn't even know existed.

There was now a newborn baby without a father. A woman, now widowed, with three kids. And me, still chasing the approval of a man who was suddenly gone forever.

Identifying his body in the morgue undid me. The tears didn't fall – they dropped like lead. Heavy. Another death. Another chapter. Another page torn from the story I'd been trying to write.

The next day, I went back to work. I buried the grief like I buried everything else, deep, out of reach, behind the gym doors and the stopwatch.

After the funeral, which hundreds attended, I

stayed in the local community, but I stepped back from the teams. For once, I couldn't pretend I was okay.

And then the real question hit me: Who am I trying to please now? He was gone. The person I'd spent a lifetime trying to impress no longer existed. And with that, a deep silence settled over me. The universe had been whispering for years through failed relationships, broken sleep, and moments of crushing emptiness: "Stop. Look inward. Ask the question." But I never did. I stayed on the move. High-functioning, high-achieving, numb. And now, there was only me.

The box of band-aids sat on my desk like a dare. I couldn't throw it out. I couldn't open it. It wasn't just a box; it was a mirror. And every time I looked at it, the same truth whispered back: "You can't outrun what you refuse to feel." But I still tried, because I wasn't ready to break the silence. Not yet.

What I didn't know then was this: The universe doesn't wait for your permission. When it decides it's time, it rips the band-aids off with no warning. And when it does, everything you have suppressed comes flooding out. Every wound. Every truth. Every scream you swallowed. You either feel it, or you break under the weight of not feeling it. My reckoning had already begun, I just hadn't heard the scream yet.

## Chapter Thirteen

# When the Band-Aids Weren't Enough

*"Until you make the unconscious conscious,
it will direct your life and you will call it fate."*
—Carl Jung

After we scattered my stepfather's ashes—his final wish, honoured in full—I thought maybe, just maybe, there'd be a moment to stop. To breathe. To reflect. But I didn't. I couldn't. So I kept rowing. Not toward anything in particular, just away from the pain. Away from the silence. The fear that if I stopped, I'd fall … and not get back up.

My connection to faith had long since burned out. Emotional awareness? Numbed. Spiritual growth? Shoved under the weight bench, collecting dust. There was no awakening on the horizon. It was just another morning, another session, another performance to curate. I was stuck in a loop of effort without evolution. Here's the hard truth that I was avoiding: without any fundamental shift, nothing fundamental would shift for me.

Olympic campaigns came and went. The work was punishing. Intense. All-consuming. The athletes carried that weight, but so did the staff, the coaches, the crew behind the curtain. Not everyone made it through.

I could still motivate others to hit peak performance – that hadn't faded. But in my personal life, I was emotionally bankrupt. I was still climbing ladders, but none of them were leading me home. I lived in extremes: full throttle or nothing. There was no gentle middle. There was no place for softness. No room to fall apart.

Professionally, I was winning. But I'd never stopped to count what I was losing along the way. The unspoken grief. The suppressed truths. The parts of myself that had quietly curled up and disappeared.

When a team lost, I would analyse everything. Break it down. Dig into the mistakes. Own what needs fixing. That level of introspection had driven my success, but I didn't know how to apply it to my own life. I didn't know how to coach "myself" through a loss, so I just kept climbing.

I took on roles overseas. They included a variety of new high-performance teams. Different arenas that had the same scoreboard: win and you're golden, lose and you're gone. The pressure was a drug. It fed my ego, it masked the silence inside, and it let me stay busy, too busy to look inward.

Leaving rowing behind was a big shift, but it was time. I found new challenges in new sports, and surrounded myself with strong people and successful campaigns. On the surface, it looked like progress, but inside, I was aching.

The void my stepfather left was vast, and I had become addicted to something I didn't yet understand: being told I wasn't good enough. He wasn't there to deliver that message anymore, so I started doing it myself. I was now repeating the old story, beating the same drum.

No personal insight, no awareness, just another loop I was stuck in.

I tried to be there for his children. They weren't biologically my family, but I felt a responsibility to show up. To make him proud. Even in death, I was still chasing his approval. When was I ever going to stop trying to earn love that could never be given?

Effort isn't intimacy. Effort isn't a connection. And I wasn't looking inward. I was outsourcing my self-worth, again.

Everything has a price. And I was paying in silence.

I entered a new relationship. This partner had children. I had another chance to be a "dad" figure, but I showed up like it was an Olympic campaign – strategic, planned, controlled. When it came to connection, in delivering emotional presence, I fell short. There was no abuse, no cruelty, but there was an absence. I wasn't "with" them. They needed love, support, presence, and I didn't have the tools.

We never asked each other the big questions, like "Why are we together? What do we believe in? What do our children need from us?"

We never built a foundation. And without a foundation, the whole thing crumbled.

And me? I had no boundaries. I couldn't say no. Not to the kids. Not to my stepfather's children. Not to anyone. I was a rubber band stretched to breaking point, too afraid that if I stood up for myself, I'd be discarded. So I kept giving, kept contorting. I kept betraying myself.

Then came a new job with a professional team. A new house. A major renovation. I should've felt proud. Settled. But my body betrayed me. I trembled. I cried, often. Surrounded by people, yet lonelier than ever. Not that they were bad people, but they weren't the right people. I had built no tribe. I did not have the right true circle of care.

My identity was tethered to "them" – the teams, the organisations, the outcomes. I stopped talking about "me," because I didn't know who that was anymore. The self-suppression program was still running. Glossy on the outside. Bleeding underneath. Then the rubber band snapped.

I kept saying yes. To the gym. To the athletes. To

the clients. To the kids. Except for myself, and what I needed, because saying no felt like a betrayal, because the boy in me still believed that letting someone down meant being left behind. I couldn't face that kind of abandonment, not from others, and not from within myself. So I overcommitted. Again, and again, and again. Until the day I forgot to pick one of the kids up after school. Not a stranger, not a client, family. I was too busy trying not to fail the world, and in doing so, I failed the ones who needed me to show up. It wasn't the first time I'd overpromised and underdelivered, either. Each slip had been forgiven. Each crack was patched over. But this one? This one snapped the rubber band.

Their mother made the call: "No more." She cut the cord, removed me from their lives, and I didn't fight it. Couldn't. Because deep down, I knew she was right. I hadn't just let them down, I'd been saying yes out of fear, not love. Fear of being abandoned again. Fear of sitting with myself. Fear of silence. Fear of all that pain waiting for me.

And the guilt? It didn't just sting, it drowned me. I tried to apologise, but silence met me outside the door.

Every step toward redemption pushed me further away. At the same time, my relationship crumbled with the person I was seeing. Another promise I couldn't keep, another structure I didn't know how to build, let alone maintain. I was neck-deep in regret, swimming through shame, and every stroke pulled me further from the shore.

I reached for help, but the help didn't fit. It spoke a language I couldn't understand. So I went back to the only place I still felt strong: work, schedules, deadlines. I pulled the mask back on, smiled through the cracks, and I pretended that I was okay. But I wasn't. The band-aids were peeling off faster than I could replace them, and beneath them, everything was bleeding.

Deep inside, a voice started to stir. A whisper. "What are you prepared to do?" It had always been there, a question I'd asked of others – of athletes, of teams. But now it turned inward. Pressing. Demanding. "What was I prepared to do to save myself?" And that whisper became a lifeline.

So I began. Slowly. Hesitantly. Small steps. I knew I needed to dig into my past, my pain, my patterns. But this wasn't surface work. It wasn't dusting the shelves. I needed a big DC-10 bulldozer. But I didn't know where to find one, or how to drive it.

The world around me kept thriving. Teams won. Businesses boomed. Everyone was rising, except me. Because no matter how much I gave, I didn't believe I was worthy of receiving.

Then something strange happened: people started showing up. I hadn't invited them. They just arrived. People who lived differently. Who had recalibrated themselves. They weren't selling anything, they were just "being". Centred. Connected. Open. Their message was simple: "Stop. Fall out of the rowing boat. Recalibrate. Learn to love yourself."

It terrified me. I was shackled to responsibility, mortgages, businesses, and teams. And fear. My ego told me that stopping meant failure. That if I paused, I'd collapse. But these people weren't speaking from theory. They were proof that healing was possible. They were living the lesson I hadn't yet learned. I listened. Not fully, but enough to plant a seed.

I wasn't ready for action. Not yet. But something was shifting. A seed had been planted. And maybe that's why the universe was getting ready to stop me, because I couldn't stop myself.

But the universe doesn't wait forever. When the whispers are ignored, it starts to shout. And if you still don't listen, it comes for you – hard, fast, and without mercy.

I didn't know it yet, but my reckoning had already begun.

## CHAPTER FOURTEEN

# When the Universe Comes for You

*"First, it whispers. Then it shouts.*
*Then it breaks you open."*

The universe had been whispering to me for years. But now, it was done whispering. It was preparing something for me – something big. I could feel it deep in my bones, like a drum beat. It was as if it were saying: 'You have so much more to give – to yourself, to others. But to unlock that, you're going to have to go through hell first."

I had spent so long asking the question "How do I connect with myself better?" But I never took the steps. I didn't do the work. I kept waiting for clarity, for permission, for a softer path forward. And so, as it always does, the universe met me where I was. It matched what I was putting out.

In my work, I attracted teams hungry to win, and I helped them win. But in my personal life, I was something else entirely: angry, frustrated, fearful, ego-driven, and underneath it all, utterly unworthy. So that's what came back to me. That's who I attracted.

My next relationship was a mirror, raw and unforgiving. This person, like me, carried a mix of fear, anger, and pain. We both wore it like a second skin. And, as before, I tried to rescue them. That was my pattern. I found women I believed needed saving. I threw myself into their fire to pull them out, because I had no idea how to rescue myself.

I didn't chase this person; they were already carrying their hurt. They spoke of experiences and people who haunted them. And I was drawn in, not because it felt right, but because it felt familiar.

Our connection wasn't grounded. It wasn't healthy. It was built on shared pain, not shared peace. And my lack of emotional awareness caused harm. I never meant to hurt anyone. But I did, because I was hurting.

Then something unexpected happened. Someone showed interest in me. They saw me. Really saw me. That had rarely happened in my life, and I didn't know what to do with it. I didn't feel worthy of it. I didn't have the tools to love myself, let alone let someone else love me. And then the universe made its first real move.

Swimming had always been my refuge. I'd swim four or five kilometres a week in the ocean, my version of pure solitude. The rhythm of the salt water on my skin, the dance of light through the waves, painting the ocean floor in moving mosaics, the sway of seaweed, the cool embrace of the current. It was peaceful.

Then, one day after a swim, I felt it: a small bump on the left side of my neck. Slight. Hard. Off. The gland was sticking out a little too far. I tried to brush it off. But something in me knew.

Within days, I was in the hands of trusted sports doctors – friends from my work. They didn't know what it was, but they got me to the right people quickly. X-rays. CT scans. Biopsies. Blood tests. No one wasted time. Soon after, I had my first operation – to remove the gland in my neck and get answers.

Then came the word I never expected. The word that brought me to my knees. "Cancer."

Even hearing it felt like swallowing broken glass. I couldn't even say it out loud. I couldn't hear this word from anyone else.

I went into denial: *This can't be happening to me.* I was fit – super fit. I could swim for kilometres, and I was able to smash out hundreds of push-ups and lead teams to win. But being fit doesn't count for much when your glands are swelling. Something was very wrong.

A second operation followed, because cancer was found at the base of my tongue. It was removed. The plan was clear: another operation to insert a feeding tube, followed by 56 brutal days of radiation and chemotherapy.

My business was shut down immediately. The door shut, just like that. No send-off. No farewell session. No time to soak in what two decades of sweat, sacrifice, and purpose had meant. One minute, I was running programs, setting schedules, and joking with clients. Next, I was gone. In a hospital gown. Prepped for surgery.

There was no space to feel it. No breath to grieve. Twenty years erased in a heartbeat, I couldn't afford to miss. I didn't get to pack the place up, shake hands, or say thanks. I didn't even get to say goodbye.

A mate of mine, more like a brother, stepped in. He was also my sub-manager, but at that moment, he became my lifeline. There wasn't enough time for planning. It was a fire sale. No dreaming of the top dollar. Just: clear it, cover the costs, and keep me alive. And he did. Every dumbbell, every bench, every bike and rowing machine was sold to fund the next incision. But what he gave me went deeper than dollars. He showed up in a way most people talk about but never do. Quiet, solid, and above all, trusting. We didn't need to say much. I simply couldn't, due to the operation on my tongue. That kind of loyalty doesn't show up often.

While the gym door slammed shut behind me, a better one had already started creaking open. I couldn't see it yet, not through the anaesthetic, not through fear, but something new had begun. Something I didn't have to lift, lead or build. Not yet. All I had to do was survive long enough to get through it.

Within myself, I was angry. Deeply, fiercely angry. Angry that I was sick. Angry that I'd let myself get here. Angry that I hadn't listened to my body, to the signs, to the people who'd tried to help me hear what the universe was sending. But this wasn't new anger – it had been building for decades. I'd had three operations in one month; my body was a war zone, and I was still trying to fight in full armour, physically, emotionally, and spiritually.

I walked into the hospital like a soldier ready for battle. Underneath, I was terrified, but my ego refused to show it. I coped the only way I knew how: by cracking jokes, making light, pretending. Humour was my smoke flare – it signalled the distress I couldn't voice.

My relationship with the head doctor of the cancer ward was somewhat challenging at the beginning of my new journey. During our first consultation, he looked at me and said, "We're going to have to nearly kill you to keep you alive." Something in me went still. It was the moment it all became real, and I hadn't "done real" for a long time, not for as long as I could remember.

I kept my cancer private. I only told a few close friends and asked them to keep it quiet. Some did. Some didn't. People's true colours showed. Some were gold. Some faded.

I reached out and called my mother. Three times. She hung up each time. Her anger, decades of it, still burned hot. I could feel it through the phone like fire. My siblings, too, carried that blaze. Only my eldest sibling stepped forward, calm and supportive.

I reached out to my biological father. His response was guarded, maybe even resentful. He said, "We're going to make sure you fight this son-of-a-bitch cancer." At that moment, I knew I didn't need another fight. I needed love, support, compassion. I did not need another battlefront. So I declined his offers. The energy didn't feel right.

These conversations gave me clarity about where everyone was on their journey. They were parked. I couldn't be.

The universe wasn't done. It sent angels, too. One of them was the nursing coordinator. She saw straight through me. She said, "You're going to be one of my most challenging patients." Then she added, "Your greatest strength will be your greatest weakness." I didn't get it at the time, but by the end of the first week of treatment, I understood.

My progress was a crawl. Painful, slow. I was admitted to the hospital again with three surgeries behind me, cancer treatment underway, a war still raging inside. My armour was crushing me; I was trying to survive behind it, but it was too heavy now. That day, I was admitted, dehydrated, disoriented and angry. I lay in a hospital bed, barely tethered to the present. A nurse leaned over, trying to insert a cannula. The first jab missed the vein. The second attempt found nothing. The third attempt was another miss. Then everything split within me. The room fractured. Shadows blurred my vision. My mind went wild with a flood of confusion. I wasn't there, but I wasn't gone either. The fear came first, then the fight. I thrashed, kicked, lashed out at people I couldn't see and all the people in my life I couldn't trust in my scrambled mind. The medical people were all trying to help. A team of six staff piled on, pinning me down as I screamed into a world that no longer made sense to me. I wasn't in control. I wasn't even in the room.

When I finally surfaced, the fight had drained from me. I lay there, shaking, sobbing, hollowed out. The sweat hadn't dried, the fear hadn't left, but something else had. The universe had arrived. Not to soothe, not to whisper, but to break me open. It tore through everything that I had suppressed and not addressed, including every mask, every band-aid, every truth I'd buried for decades. There was no performance left. No title. No role. No identity. No words to hide behind. Just breath. Just pain. Just the truth. And in that present moment, I didn't surrender with grace, or strength. I surrendered by falling apart, physically, emotionally, mentally, and spiritually. Utterly.

The universe wasn't gentle. It wasn't soft. But it was precise. Clear. Unforgiving in its mercy. It didn't whisper. It meant business. It peeled back every layer, slowly, deliberately, until I was heaving on the hospital floor, naked in the wreckage of everything I'd refused to face. Raw. Exposed. Terrified. But beneath the fear, something stirred. It was preparing me, not for a comeback, not to lead, not to save someone else, but to finally stop pretending. To stop fixing. To stop running. To begin, not again, but for real. From the inside out. To finally start healing the one person I had always abandoned: me. I had never truly surrendered. Not to love, not to pain, and not to the truth. But now, there was no more hiding. The universe had stopped whispering – it was roaring. And this time, when it asked "What are you prepared to do?", I was sitting up, finally ready to listen. But I had no idea that listening would mean losing everything I thought made me strong—my voice, my body, my independence, my mask—until only the real me was left.

That's where the real story began: not with a battle, but with surrender.

## Chapter Fifteen

# The Real Power of Surrender

*"Surrender is not giving up.*
*It is letting go of the illusion of control."*

My surrender wasn't a weakness – it was the moment I stopped clinging and started listening. It was the invitation I didn't ask for, delivered by cancer, to shed every illusion I had of strength, and finally see the real thing. I'd built my whole life on control, performance, pace, perseverance. I knew how to lead, protect, and fix. I didn't know how to receive it. Or fall apart. Or ask.

By the first week of treatment, that illusion crumbled. My throat was a war zone. It felt like a road train had parked itself there and refused to move. And with it, my voice, which was all but gone. The very thing I'd used to prove I mattered, to command rooms, to hide the pain. Just like that, it was silenced.

I had to learn how to speak through my eyes.

Through listening. Through being still. I had to learn how to feel, without translating it into action or performance. Something in me had to end so something else could begin.

I realised that I thought I'd lost something, but what I was gaining was everything.

Radiation entered me like a ghost – just seconds a day, but it haunted every cell. Chemotherapy crept drip by drip through my veins, while a tube, nicknamed "Jake the Peg", hung from my stomach, feeding me what I could no longer take by mouth. Jake and I didn't start on the best of terms, but over time, he became more than a tube. He became a symbol, a companion, a strange, silent witness to my unravelling, and my rebirth.

Each day was a lesson in loss. Each moment was a chance to let go.

My body shrank – once 75 kilograms, to 49. My skin stretched across my bones. I was a ghost in the mirror.

Sitting in the shower took the same energy as a rowing final. The water hit like needles. My plastic shower chair became my throne of surrender. And yet – inside? Inside, something sacred was unfolding. With all my usual scaffolding stripped away, I began to meet myself. Not the coach. Not the performer. Just "me". Raw, vulnerable, and human. I learned about self-love, worthiness, and boundaries. I learned to trust my gut, not just metaphorically, but literally. It was my gut, after all, that was now keeping me alive.

I started asking myself "What are you prepared to do?" But not in the way I used to. Not as a challenge, but as a companion, a compass. A gentle call inward. I built myself a ritual. Something small, something of mine. I called it "the 2 × 1". Each day, I'd name two things I was doing well, and one thing I wanted to invest in. Some days, the bar was low: "I'm breathing." I'm blinking." That was enough. That was everything.

At night, when the world went still, the real shadows came. The shadows you could not see. Not just the ones outside the window, but the ones that were lurking through the cracks in my mind. I'd lie there, whispering my 2 × 1s into the silence, as tears traced slow lines down my face, tiny proof I was still here. I was contributing to myself.

Around me in the shared ward, others were breaking. Screaming. Hallucinating. Their armour was being removed slowly. Nurses rushed in, five, six at a time, to calm, restrain, and soothe.

The nights belonged to ghosts. To pain. To those of us crossing invisible bridges between past, body, and soul. In the midst of it all, I kept asking: "What are you prepared to do?" And for the first time, the answer came back without punishment or pressure: "Love myself. Ask for help. Let it in."

That alone was a revolution. Before, I had never felt worthy of asking for help. Now, I had no choice. And slowly, it stopped feeling like a weakness, and started to feel like courage.

I didn't accept many visitors. I was unable to speak, and I couldn't afford them. It was not that I didn't want them, but that the ones who came left shaken, my energy too fragile to host or protect "them". So I stopped. I prioritised myself. Still, cards arrived from across the world. And this time, I let the love in. I did not just read the cards – I received everything on the card. And for the first time in my life, I believed I deserved it.

One day, my older sibling came. We didn't trade accomplishments. We didn't try to impress. We just were. In the absence of armour, we met each other again, heart to heart, not head to head. Few words, but more meaning than we'd shared in years.

Then came the angels. That's what I called them. The unexpected messengers who showed up just when I needed something my soul hadn't dared ask for.

Every day, blood was drawn from my black, bruised, punctured arms. The phlebotomists were called "vampires" by some, but to me, they were lifelines. They were looking for one number: my white blood cell count. If it dropped below 1%, treatment would have to pause.

One morning, a new face appeared. Dark-skinned. Spanish accent. Quiet hands. Gentle eyes. He took my blood with unusual grace. There were no words exchanged, just a mutual understanding. I thanked him silently with my eyes. He left. Then, minutes later, he returned. I was slumped low in bed. Voiceless. Too weak to raise my head. He stood beside me, locked eyes with me, and said, "You're going to be alright. "You will be all right." He paused. "You just have to believe."

I grabbed my notepad and scribbled, "Believe in what? God? Hope? What do I believe in?"

He looked at it, smiled gently, and said, "You just have to believe in yourself." And he walked out. I never saw him again.

Days later, I asked the nurse coordinator if she could thank the Spanish blood tech. She checked the chart. "No one by that name or description has been on this ward," she said. "No one with a Spanish accent. No one in this section." She flipped through the pages again. "Nothing. No record."

I knew, in my bones, that he was sent by something bigger. And this moment, this visitor, cracked open something inside me. He didn't just insert a needle – he delivered a message straight into my soul. It wasn't religion. It wasn't fantasy. It was real. And it changed everything.

For all the weight I'd lost, I'd gained something weightless, but powerful: I'd learned to surrender. Not as a defeat, but as freedom. The kind of surrender that doesn't strip you of your dignity, but returns it. The kind that says: "You don't have to carry everything anymore." That "You are already enough. Just as you are." To "Let go. Let love in. Trust."

That's when I truly began to heal. That's when I truly began to live. And when I finally let go, it wasn't silence I found, it was a signal, a whisper from somewhere beyond pain and noise: "You're not done yet."

As the ward dimmed, and the machines hummed their last lullaby, something stirred deep inside me. The light was coming back. Not in grand explosions, not in triumph. In something smaller. Simpler. In flavour. In memory. In a custard tart.

# Chapter Sixteen

## Custard Tart and the Stars

*"Sometimes it's not the taste that returns*
*– it's the will to live that sneaks in with it."*

The medical team would place a bright yellow gel in my mouth a couple of times a day; it was meant to manage the phlegm and the relentless coughing that came with the treatment. The phlegm, they said, was a good sign. It meant the chemo was doing its job. I'd done plenty of sit-ups over the years, but this was something else entirely. Each cough was a body blow. Like being punched from the inside out. My stomach muscles were scorched, so raw I could barely shift in bed. And every time my body heaved, I could feel Jake the Peg rattling under the strain. Sometimes I wondered how I hadn't coughed him clean out of me, but somehow, he kept hanging on, a cough at a time. It was brutal, but it was also a strange kind of reassurance. The pain meant I was still here, still conscious, still alive.

On the final day of treatment, they placed the same yellow gel in my mouth, but this time I could taste it: custard tart, of all things.

I'd given more than a few custard tarts a nudge in my day, but this was different. This was a miracle in disguise. I scribbled the words *custard tart* on my notepad and showed them to the nursing coordinator. Her face lit up. Not just a smile, not just a look of relief, or hope, or joy. Her whole body responded as if she had just received the best news of the week. She knew what it meant. Taste returning during treatment was "almost unheard of." And somehow, my body had listened. Those endless wheelchair laps through the hospital cafeteria, rolling past food I couldn't eat, conjuring flavours I could barely remember, they hadn't been for nothing. I'd sit there, the food displays in front of me, staring at a plate I couldn't touch, tasting with my mind instead. Letting memory do the work. Letting imagination stir something my body had nearly forgotten. Flavour. Desire. Life. Now, my body whispered: "You're coming back."

The radiation mask came off for the last time that afternoon. There was a faint, exhausted sense of celebration, but I knew the truth: treatment had ended, but recovery had only just begun.

No more radiation. No more chemo. No more blood tests into bruised, collapsing veins. No more screams in the night. No more sterile antiseptic smells. No more cafeteria visualisation tours. No more blue-buttoned pyjamas.

No more wonderful, caring hospital staff to joke with and lean on.

I was supposed to leave the next day. Then the blood results came in. My white blood cell count had collapsed. I was neutropenic. "Under 1." Dangerously exposed. Fragile. Weak. I weighed 49kg and could barely stand.

Jake, the feeding tube, was still riding shotgun. I couldn't eat solids; I could barely swallow water. Leaving that hospital felt like leaving the air itself, but the nursing coordinator looked at me and said something I'll never forget: "You're not going to get better in here. You've got to leave here to get better."

I nodded. But inside, I was screaming.

I'd become institutionalised. The hospital was my world. The system had wrapped around me like a womb. I didn't know how to exist without it.

Then life, true to form, intervened. I was moved into isolation. Room #3. I chose it because I remembered it as the lucky one. People got wheeled into those rooms and didn't always come out. But I did. For nearly three weeks, it became my home. No visitors. No walks. Just me, the sterile walls, and the deep echoing quiet. But I was still alive. And I had a choice: to wait … or to begin.

I didn't waste a second. I turned that little room into

a command centre of transformation. I delivered as many 2 × 1s to myself as I could, shifting my thinking from "victim" to "visionary." I journaled. I imagined. I made maps of my life after the hospital. And gratitude returned like a long-lost friend. So did hope.

When the time finally came to leave, the whole medical team came to see me off. They hadn't just watched a man survive – they'd witnessed a man strip himself bare, peel back and remove every resource he'd ever used to cover pain. They saw what it meant to face suffering head-on and keep walking.

I didn't go back to my place in the bay. I didn't have the strength. Instead, close friends dropped me off at a mate's house, who generously opened it for me. I arrived there with nothing but bones, silence, and a plastic tube in my stomach. Spiritually, physically, emotionally, I had hit rock bottom, but the beautiful thing about rock bottom is this: there's only one way left – up.

That first night out of the hospital, I lay metaphorically face down in the gutter. I could almost feel the cold concrete pressing into my cheek. Rough. Indifferent. Then I rolled over. And looked up. The stars were still there. They hadn't left. Not once. Not even when I forgot they existed.

I wept. Not from pain, but from the miracle of noticing. From gratitude. From the ache of beauty I'd once taken for granted.

Adjusting to life outside was strange. Unsteady. I was still with Jake, who performed nightly with stoic devotion. The streets felt alien. People moved too fast. Everything felt overwhelming. I bought a small cup of watermelon juice. It was coarse and rough, but I held onto that cup all day. I sipped it slowly. Reverently. Each mouthful felt like a conversation with life itself. I still couldn't drink mineral water, but I'd hold it in my mouth, feel the tiny bubbles dance and burst on my tongue, then spit it out. Joy wasn't just possible, it was tactile. Immediate. Real.

The house I stayed in was full of world travellers. They were light, free, full of stories. No expectations. No pity. Just movement, laughter, and colour. I needed that energy. Some of the medical team even visited. They said they missed me. I missed them too.

Eventually, I began a small routine: wake up at 7 am; walk down the private laneway; stretch in the morning sun for fifteen minutes; a breakfast of watered-down egg smoothies with Jake's help; check emails; read the news; rest. It felt like I was slowly rebuilding something.

Then one morning, the police were waiting at the end of the lane. Three uniformed officers, one plainclothes detective. They questioned me:

"Where do you live?"

"What are you doing here?"

"Show us your arms."

To them, I was a pale skeleton in a hoodie. A ghost

with haunted eyes and bruised veins. They saw a junkie. They couldn't hear my voice; it was too damaged to speak clearly. I wrote most of my answers on paper. But even as they read my words, they didn't believe me. They wanted proof. I told them to follow me back to the house. The challenge was that it was uphill. I needed to rest constantly. My legs were like reeds.

Then Jake made his move. The medical tape had loosened. He flopped under my shirt like he sometimes did, playful and erratic. I lifted my shirt. There he was, Jake, the PEG tube. Swinging proudly in the sunlight like some strange badge of honour.

Their faces turned white. Shock. Disbelief. Horror. The tone shifted instantly. Business cards. Apologies. Offers of help. Jake had cleared my name. But he wasn't done teaching me yet.

A few days later, the skin around him flared up, red, angry, and infected. The grommet under my skin had rubbed too much. It was painful. Hot to the touch. My gut feelings were sending me a message via Jake. The old me would've ignored it. I would have powered through. The new me? I went straight to the hospital.

The local ER rushed me in. The doctor was Irish. Thick accent. No Guinness, but a challenge to understand. He asked how I spent my day, which I shared with him. He listened, inspected and frowned. Then said something that cut straight through me: "That routine you have is killing Jake. Never go back to a routine again."

His treatment was to bathe Jake in hot, salty water. He told me to drop the routine and to come back and see him in two weeks. I followed it religiously, and in that unexpected rebellion from structure, I began to trust something I hadn't trusted in a long time: my gut" Not just the physical gut, but the *knowing* that lives deep inside it. The part that whispers, "You're ready." The part that says, "Let go." The part that points upward when you're lying face down in the gutter.

Jake had once fed me nutrition. Now, he was feeding something deeper: instinct, intuition, inner trust. And just like that, I began to heal.

When I looked up at the stars that night, I wasn't just seeing light. I was seeing the parts of me that had survived.

I wasn't sure where this road would take me, but I knew one thing: I wasn't going back, not to who I was, not to how I lived, and not to what nearly killed me.

The stars had stayed. Now it was my turn. To rise. To walk. To live a new way, on the right path.

CHAPTER SEVENTEEN

# The Healing Road

*"You do not heal from trauma.*
*You simply come to know yourself as someone other*
*than the person defined by it."* —Dr. Gabor Maté

Each day of healing was a slow, sacred act of rebellion, and it was extremely challenging at times. Rebellion against the way I had always lived: driven, performing, fixing. But I wasn't sprinting anymore. I wasn't performing. I was learning to *be*, to live *with* myself, not despite myself. And for the first time, that question, the one that had driven me for years, returned with new gravity: "What are you prepared to do?"

I was prepared to live. To live differently. To choose presence over performance. Stillness over speed. Being over becoming. Allowing over trying. And so, I started small.

I woke when my body asked me to, not when clocks or alarms insisted. I ate when hunger arrived, not when the world told me to. I slept when exhaustion came, and for once, I didn't feel guilty for resting. This slow, strange rhythm initially felt selfish. But it wasn't. It was essential. It was survival redefined.

I changed my menu – yes, my food menu, now fully organic, but also the menu of my mind. No more sugar-coated distractions. No more numbing out. No chocolate either – I couldn't swallow it. My dry mouth turned every craving into a quiet lesson.

The band-aids were off. I was exposed. Raw. And for the first time, I wasn't running from that. I was sitting *with* it. I was allowing it to teach me. I felt like the new kid at school, dumped into a curriculum of survival I'd never studied before.

The side effects from treatment weren't over. I couldn't produce saliva. My temperature would spike without warning, leaving me soaked in sweat. Fatigue would land like an ambush. My speech faltered. But behind every setback was something else: an invitation to deepen. To learn patience. To practice compassion. To sit with uncertainty and still say: this is my path, I will walk it, and I will be okay.

I called in every support tool available: acupuncture, yoga, lymphatic massage, speech therapy, improved dental care, incredible counselling, meditation, journaling, medication, swims in the ocean and slow walks in nature. Each was a ritual. A recovery and discovery ritual.

Somewhere in there, I allowed strength in surrendering. And then came a quiet but profound moment: the day Jake had to depart me.

Jake wasn't just a feeding tube. He was a lifeline, sure, but somewhere along the way, he'd become something stranger. Quirky. Almost companion-like. A silent witness, an unsung hero to every rise and fall on the cancer journey.

I asked the nurse to hold my hand. I requested her to bring tissues. I knew why I was emotional: because Jake had done more than keep me alive. He'd let nourishment in when I couldn't swallow. He'd nudged me, gently, insistently, when infection flared, reminding me to loosen my grip on routine. He'd stepped up as interpreter when the police came knocking, popping out like a weird, defiant badge of truth. And he'd tangled himself, often, just for laughs.

He reminded me, over and over, that survival wasn't neat. It was messy. Unpredictable. Sometimes even a little ridiculous, laced with his unique brand of quirky humour. And now, his time was done. No more taping him down. No more navigating showers with care. No more half-sleep from the awkward pull of plastic snaking from my stomach.

His removal marked more than a medical milestone. It was a turning point. The end of dependence. Another step forward on the road to recovery. A quiet, strange farewell to a companion I never asked for, but will never forget, thanks to the small scar, a little badge of honour he left behind. A reminder. A signature. Proof that we'd made it together.

I could sleep on my side again. I could breathe without pain. And every night, I rinsed my mouth, because saliva no longer came. Each small act, each swallow, each breath, was now holy.

I became quieter. I spoke less. Listened more. Slept in stillness. The new rhythms settled in. Not always comfortably, but honestly.

I reached out to my siblings. I wanted to share my aliveness, not just as a survival, but as a celebration. I hoped they might meet me there, in that spirit. As the conversations unfolded, it became painfully clear: most of them were still stuck. Emotionally parked. Their hearts still scattered like debris from our family story, too painful to retrieve, too haunting to revisit. I couldn't fix them. Not anymore. I didn't have the energy. I was learning to live my life with my new healthy boundaries, so I could only offer presence, delivering this to them as a quiet beacon.

Healing is a solo invitation. I opened the door for them all; they have to choose to walk through.

My parents? Silence. I'd stopped expecting anything. That, too, was healing. Low expectations are a powerful medicine. They release you from resentment. So, instead of blaming, I sent out compassion like a message in a bottle.

I hope and pray that one day, it will reach their shore.

The relationship I was in had shifted, too. We'd started the journey together, but I'd taken a plunge inward that had changed everything. I was swimming in new waters now, speaking a language of vulnerability, self-awareness, and surrender, but the person beside me hadn't heard the call. They were paused. Parked. Perhaps they were unaware, or even lost in their challenges. I wasn't diving in to fix them anymore. My old rescue kit, once always within arm's reach, was gone. I wasn't the rescuer now. I was the recoverer.

I still cared deeply. Trusted them. That mattered. Trust was sacred. Rare. But trust couldn't carry a person not willing to move with it. So I did the only thing I could: I let go with love. Then came a moment of clarity.

One morning, full of appreciation—for breath, for blinking, for taste, for movement—I climbed into my 1968 VW Beetle. The engine purred like an old friend, and the whisper came: "Why not go? Why not create space to heal, fully, deliberately, wildly?"

So I did.

I packed light: a two-man tent, coconut water, a tiny travel bag, and a willingness
to listen to the land. My medical team approved it, as long as I came back monthly.

I hit the road. Driving slowly, at a top speed of 70 km/h, meant the whole world had no choice but to slow down with me.

My little Beetle wasn't just a transport; it became a curiosity. People honked and waved as they passed. A meditation on wheels. A rolling metaphor for everything I was learning to live again.

Road trains thundered past. Kangaroos bounded by. Camels, goats, emus, and blowflies all overtook me without a second glance, and in their dusty wake, the universe handed me something I didn't even realise I was starving for: space to see. To really see.

I pulled over often. Not because I had to, but because I could. By rivers that flowed with no agenda. Beneath ghost gums that had witnessed more than I ever would. On red tracks that vanished into the horizon and disappeared into silence. I snapped iPhone photos, not for likes or proof, but to honour the moment. I scribbled in my journal, not a to-do list, but slow, meandering reflections of what I was receiving.

This wasn't about getting anywhere fast. It wasn't a performance. It was a presence. I simplified everything. If I was tired, I rested. If I felt strong, I drove. No pressure. No striving. No interruptions or distractions. Just having enough awareness to listen to what my body was saying to me.

The road became my therapist. The dust, my medicine. The silence, my teacher. And in that stillness, something extraordinary happened: I reconnected with myself – not the man I'd performed as, but the one who'd been there all along. The one who never needed fixing, only remembering.

People smiled longer. Conversations lingered. And so did I. But I was still healing. Still raw. I was still bandage-free. And with that openness, sometimes dust blew into the wounds. But that, too, was part of it. Healing doesn't always look like light pouring through a window. Sometimes, it's standing in red dirt with tears in your eyes and your hands in your pockets, whispering, "Thank you for this experience." Because this road wasn't just a journey through Australia. It was a pilgrimage. A reclamation. A new methodology for living.

I wasn't running or hiding anymore. I was finally being. And for the first time in a long time, I wasn't just surviving – I was healing. Slowly. Deeply. The right way for me.

But the road wasn't done with me yet. Because sometimes, just when you think you've found peace, life hands you a deeper invitation. The kind that cracks the heart open all over again, not to break it, but to let more light in.

# The Light Beyond the Wounds

*"The wound is the place where the Light enters you."*
—Rumi

There were three of us were on that road: the car, the land, and me. And we weren't travelling – we were transforming. Somewhere between the red dust plains and ocean-backed cliffs, we stopped being separate entities. We blurred into one story. One skin. And with each kilometre, the noise faded. Time didn't tick anymore, it opened. I didn't measure it. I welcomed it. There was one question echoing louder than ever: "What are you prepared to do?" To contribute, not just outwardly, but inwardly. To yourself. Your soul. Your truth.

I began sharing my story in fragments. Small reflections posted online – no filters, no advice, just raw, lived truth. At first, twenty people followed. Then two hundred. Once the chapter titled 'Bundy, Boxing and the Beaver' was sent out about the adventures of the last boxing troupe in the country, the readership went to thousands. By the time the old VW and I rolled into the far north, five thousand people were tuning in from across the world.

But it was never about the car, or the map. It was about connection, the kind only truth can unlock. The kind that says, "I see you. I'm with you. I've been there too."

Every post became a mirror. No answers. No telling, no offerings. And somehow, just by showing up honestly, something changed. It made a difference. Even the head nurse at one of my hospital check-ups said, "Those posts are helping more patients than you'll ever know." And that's when I understood: Nothing of real value means much unless it's shared.

That journey created something beautiful: a picture book, built from those reflections. Three hundred pages, part story, part soul. I co-created it with the person I was seeing at the time. It sold more than 5,000 copies, and raised funds for others on their cancer path. That felt like light returned to the world, but the person I was seeing couldn't share in the joy. They didn't seem proud, or grateful, or present. To them, it was just a book. To me, it was meaning. It was healing made visible. Yet they kept pulling away. Not always with words, but in the pauses. When I reached for their hand, they didn't connect back. When I moved in for a hug, their body stayed stiff, arms slow to follow. When I stood beside them in public, they wouldn't find the words to call me their partner.

It wasn't rejection in loud, obvious ways. It was in the quiet hesitations. The empty space where closeness should've lived. The kind of silence that says everything.

Still, I invited them to be part of the next chapter: a return journey, this time to the spiritual heart of the country. Out there, the land doesn't speak – it sings. The air is sacred, and the ground hums. The silence stretches into you until you remember who you are.

I filmed it, and produced my first short film. I edited with this person who understood what I was experiencing in my life at the time, and I titled it *The Right Path*. Because no one came with me. Not once. Not even for a moment. They had their distractions; I had my purpose and my truth.

When I came home, they told me they no longer wanted to be part of my life. That's when it tore two ancient wounds I thought had healed: truth and trust. Those two wounds were still open. I didn't see it coming, and the grief hit like surfacing too fast from a deep dive: I was dizzy, disoriented, dismantled.

I thought I was past trauma responses, but that old, familiar terror came back like a long-lost friend. They couldn't hear my truth, but what I couldn't see at the time was that they were sadly drowning in their own. That moment, as painful as it was, wasn't really about me. It was about their wounds. Their pain. Their lack of awareness and refusal to face the mirror. But for me? This wasn't just heartbreak. It was initiation.

I had cared deeply. Once again, I had loved someone carrying my mother's patterns: emotionally absent, unable to see themselves, projecting their pain instead of processing it.

That was my addiction – not to chaos, but to the hope that I could heal someone else before I healed myself.

This was the universe was taking me by the shoulders and whispering. "It's time to stop bleeding for people who won't even look at their wounds. It's time to address this addiction "

So I didn't reach for the band-aids or a mask. I did not suppress, but stayed open to address what was needed. I let it burn. And when it got dark, which it did many times, I stayed disciplined. I asked myself again: "What are you prepared to do?" And this time, the answer was clear: "Anything."

I found healers. Not practitioners, not influencers, but healers. Some lived high in the mountains, quiet as the wind. Others came from overseas, brought by fate, not plans.

They didn't give answers; they held space. They helped me remember what was mine, and what never was.

Some friends couldn't go there with me. They offered half-truths and hollow encouragement:

"Harden up."

"You'll find someone else."

"You got to move on."

"Watch porn."

"Get a new counsellor."

They meant well, but I couldn't walk backwards anymore to keep them comfortable.

Others did show up. With questions, not answers. With fair dinkum scars, not borrowed theories. With a presence that felt like a prayer.

My tribe became fewer, but truer.

My older sibling showed up for part of the journey, and I was deeply grateful. Because this wasn't a retreat. It was a reckoning. The curriculum? Patience. Self-kindness. Radical honesty. And above all: love that starts within.

Then I saw the pattern. The magnetic pull I'd always had to the unavailable. I wasn't cursed – I was repeating. But now, I had the strength to do what few ever do: break the cycle.

This wasn't just about healing a broken heart, but about healing a broken pattern. And to do that, I had to say yes to the deepest thing I'd ever said yes to: me. So I read. I walked alone. I cried. I forgave. I excavated old family stories buried in shame and silence.

Sometimes, I wanted to reach for something numbing. A lie. A distraction. Another band-aid. A comfortable half-life. But I didn't, because for the first time, I wanted to feel. Even the grief. Especially the grief.

I was fortunate, as the universe delivered my requests, and was able to I feel all the grief. And there, beneath the rubble, It appeared: my purpose. Not what I do, but who I am.

I named my values. I meet with my inner archetypes. I redefined communication with myself and others. I stopped performing my boundaries and started living them. And I gave myself something no one else had ever truly given me: freedom. Freedom from seeking. Freedom from proving. Freedom from the fear of not being enough.

I walk differently now. Not perfect, but present. I carry compassion, not shame. Authenticity, not performance. And an unwavering commitment to contribute to me first, so I can serve from wholeness, not from wounds.

That one question, What are you prepared to do? It's no longer a challenge. It's a compass. One that keeps pointing me in the right direction. And as I write this, I can't help but think of my younger brother. If he'd known how much light was entering his wounds, not just pain, but light, I wonder if he might still be here. Maybe he couldn't see it or feel it. Maybe no one ever showed him how. But I see it now. I feel it. And I'll carry it for both of us.

I am not the man who started that journey. To become this man, I had to pass through fire, flood, and finally, stillness. And on that road, I found not just healing, but transformation.

This is the hero's journey. Not because I conquered anything, but because I remembered who I've always been. I am free, not because nothing hurts anymore, but because I let it all in, and lived.

I thought I had found the light beyond the wound, but what came next would show me this: healing isn't the end of the journey – it's the beginning of the reckoning. And reckoning doesn't wait for permission.

# The Reckoning and the Road

*"You are the hero you've been waiting for."*

What are you prepared to do? This question has followed me for as long as I can remember. It's crossed oceans with me. It's echoed down sterile hospital corridors. Sat silently in high-performance teams and boardrooms. It's walked beside me through victory parades and solitary hungover mornings after. It's outlasted the applause of wins, the ache of losses, the sting of betrayal, and the long, private challenge of healing.

What are you prepared to do?

It's not a slogan. Not a motivational catchphrase. It's a mirror. And it doesn't ask for an answer. It asks for honesty. Not in theory. In practice. When the plan falls apart, which it will at times. When your body gives way. When the version of you that held everything together begins to crack. It found me in all those places and let the light in. And when I stopped running, side-stepping, ducking, weaving and suppressing, I realised I'd been carrying that question, and avoiding it, for many years.

I didn't write this memoir to relieve my pain. I wrote it because I'm aware that I'm still learning from it. Not to grow old, but to grow up from it. Because the road didn't end at the breakthrough, it just changed direction. Because even now, I'm still asking that same question. Only these days, I ask it from a place of stillness, not survival. Not from fear.

I've moved through rage, shame, guilt, confusion, love, loss, joy, and grace. I've worn masks so long that I forgot what my face looked like. I've chased gold stars, over-delivered, people-pleased, and powered through, until there was nothing left to power with. Until I was completely running on empty. And then, slowly, I started to become aware and listen. To the silence. To the grief, I buried myself under goals. To the anger, I wrapped myself in humour. To the emptiness, I tried to outwork. And in that quiet, when the universe delivered it, something shifted. Not all at once. Ever so slowly. Not perfectly. But deeply. Very gently. Like the land, when it changes seasons.

I started showing up differently. Not to impress, just to be present. Not with answers, just with my full self. That was the turning point. There's a kind of strength that isn't loud. It doesn't need fixing or framing. It just ... is. It's when you can look in the mirror, after the fall, after the loss, after the illusion's gone, and say, "I'm still here.

And I'm not abandoning myself." That's the kind of strength I'm allowing myself to live into now. Not preach. Not perform. Just live.

Maybe your story is nothing like mine. But maybe you've felt something similar. The pull to be more than what you've survived. The ache of carrying a story that no one else quite understands. The quiet longing to be known, really known and still loved anyway. If so, I get it. I'm still figuring it out, too. This chapter, this book, isn't a formula. It's not a lesson plan. It's just a fire I built from all the wreckage, believing the warmth will reach someone else.

These pages were never about telling you what to do. They were about showing you where I've been. And if there's something in them that echoes something in you, then maybe that's enough. That's a contribution to you.

Some days I still reach for the old armour. The performance. The proving. Now, I notice the awareness I have. Now, I pause. Now, I become present. To the truth. To my breath. To the ground beneath my feet. Because presence doesn't always roar. Sometimes, it just whispers, "This moment is enough. You are enough. Have another go again, with no armour this time."

I don't know where you are in your own story. Maybe you're still trying to find your footing. Maybe you're quietly tired of waiting for permission to live the way you were meant to.

I've been there. I still visit sometimes. As a visitor, then I depart. But if there's one thing I keep learning, it's this: the next step doesn't need to be dramatic, it just needs to be true, and it needs to be yours.

The people who matter—your kids, your friends, and your crew—they don't need

your perfection. They need your presence. They need you real. That's what I'm still learning to give. How lucky am I?

So I'll leave you with the same question that still shapes every day of my life – not

as a command, but as an offering of a gift: What are you prepared to do? Not for your ego. Not for the cameras. Not for the trophies. Not even for the identity you've spent years building. But for peace. For the purpose. For the parts of you still waiting to be seen. For the story of my life, which I am ever so grateful for, that still has so much left to give.

Because, as I discovered, it's never too late to come home to yourself.

And it's never too soon to begin.